Counting Heads

COUNTING HEADS

The Collected Works of

Susan J. Gordon

For Edward and Peter, my splendid sons who inspired me to write these stories, and also starred in many of them. My pride in you is boundless; raising you, and being your mom has been the best thing I've done!

TABLE OF CONTENTS

INTRODUCTION

LOVE AND MARRIAGE

FAMILY MATTERS

PARENTHOOD

ONE FAMILY'S BACK PAGES

SHINING STARS

KEYS TO HOME

FICTION

ACKNOWLEDGMENTS

"Write it down. Just write it down," I told myself. I was about twelve years old, and knew if I wrote down what I was thinking, I could keep it, save it, and read it later or anytime I wanted.

That year, for my birthday, next-door neighbors had given me a diary—a private place to write and say anything. I was thrilled, and I was hooked on recording my thoughts and my words.

Over the years, many people have read my published stories, which are now collected here. Special thanks go to my husband, Ken, who still proofreads everything and comments (wisely, and usually gently, for which I am grateful), his terrific assistant Holly Staver, my sons and daughters-in-law Edward and Patrice, Peter and Melissa, my Petkun cousins, my late brother Mike Dyer, and late sister-in-law Carol Dyer, as well as my late mother and her two late sisters—my wonderful aunts—I miss them all. Also, I am thankful for Rabbi Shira Milgrom, and dear friends who continue to this day to encourage me and champion my work: Gail Gitman, Pat Tomassi, Elaine Klein, My and Minh Duong, and Irma Olmedo Williams.

In addition, I am deeply appreciative for the help and support of the Authors Guild, especially Johnny Chinnici, Marketing and Communications Coordinator of the Guild, who has shepherded this book, as well as my earlier book, *WEDDING DAYS: When & How Great Marriages Began* (2020), through the Guild's Back-in-Print program.

INTRODUCTION

A Writer's Reflections

by Anne Garry,
Managing Editor, *Victoria Magazine*

"Inspired by treasured family memories and musings, Susan J Gordon's work strikes a chord of connection in the hearts of her many readers."

For many who choose writing as a profession, the decision is not made definitely until their college years. But this career path seemed almost predestined for Susan J. Gordon, a prolific essayist based in White Plains, New York. Her work has been published in a variety of national magazines and newspapers.

"Even as a young girl—long before I ever thought that I would become a published author—writing was my way of making sense out of things," she says. "Putting my thoughts into worthwhile and clear sentences helps me figure out how I feel, and this has helped me make meaningful changes in my life."

Many of Susan's early childhood experiences were instrumental in shaping her lifelong love of the written word, an appreciation that the budding scribe came by naturally. "I grew up in my grandmother's small apartment, where my mother took my older brother and me after she divorced my father. Although our living quarters were tight, bookshelves dominated the living room," Susan recalls. "Sometimes in the evenings, after I was in bed and my mother had come home from work, she'd sit quietly at the kitchen table and read passages aloud from Shakespeare's plays. The apartment would be filled with the soothing sounds of her voice."

Family and her Jewish heritage have proven to be predominant themes of Susan's work, inspiring her to embark on a personal journey during which she tracked down family members in Budapest and Ukraine. During her travels, she also visited the ancestral homes of several of her relatives who had lived and died during World War II and the Holocaust.

"The past is always present, I believe, whether or not we're conscious of it," she says. "My curiosity intensified in the past ten years when I realized that the older people in my family were dying; if I didn't ask questions now, I never could. That's when I began to actively pursue family-tree research."

The information Susan gleaned through her genealogical studies motivated her to author a series of detailed family histories. Her current work in progress, a memoir entitled *Because of Eva*, is the fascinating story of Susan's 90-year old second cousin, whom she located in Tel Aviv in 1999. Eva had cared for Susan's grandfather who had died thirty years before, and when Susan made the trip to thank her, she learned much about Eva's bravery and strength during the 1944 German occupation of Budapest.

Susan also was successful in finding the birth, marriage, and death records of her great-grandparents and other ancestors.

She continues to find great inspiration from her immediate family. Susan has written essays reminiscing about raising her two now-adult sons, and her marriage of more than forty years played a role in her decision to write the book, *Wedding Days: When and How Great Marriages Began.*

"Both my husband and I grew up in families of divorce, so we knew that having a good marriage required effort and commitment, passion and abiding love," she says. "Part of me has always been fascinated by other people's marriages—seeing how they worked and how they didn't."

Wedding Days contains 366 romantic, humorous, and surprising stories about how famous couples met, wooed, and wed. For example, the book reveals that the inventor Thomas Edison proposed marriage to Mina Miller by tapping "Will you marry me?" in the palm of her hand using Morse Code because her overbearing parents would not leave the couple alone. And when the future French emperor Napoleon married Josephine, his bride insisted that her ill-tempered pug sleep with them on their wedding night.

Speaking on television and radio shows about the topics of love and marriage, Susan firmly maintains that "the concept of romance in our society is not obsolete; many people yearn for it. But sometimes we get distracted by the trappings of romance instead of the essence, which is more about constancy, devotion, and love."

No matter the topic, for Susan, the most important goal is to connect with her readers. "What's wonderful for me is that, through my published work, people can relate to my feelings, even if they haven't had the same experiences," she says.

Victoria — January/February 2009

COUNTING HEADS, AND MAKING SENSE

Thank you, dear readers, for your interest in my work! I have always been thrilled to see my words in print—no matter how much or how little I was paid. To quote the late comedian Henny Youngman, when I interviewed him for *Wedding Days*, "never write anything unless they pay you for it!"

Most of the pieces are about universal topics such as marriage, family life, parenting, being Jewish, and family histories, and were written for well-known, popular publications including *American Baby*, *Brides*, *Family Circle*, *Good Housekeeping*, *Lilith*, *Parents*, *Victoria*, *Woman's Day*, *Working Mother*, the *Jewish Week of New York*, and the *New York Times*.

Most of the titles of the stories which follow were chosen by my editors—the good people who accepted my work and published it in their magazines, newspapers, and online sites.

Altogether, you might say this collection is the story of a family in the late 20th century. Topics range from serious ones such as stepfathers (maligned, too often, and not cheered enough), unending anti-Semitism, and remembering (and giving thanks for) the restorative value of ordinary days... to humorous ones including those about car pooling, packing the summer camp trunk, and scraping wax off a Chanukah menorah.

Childhood, I have learned, is as fleeting as falling leaves, and home is where you can find your way in the dark. There are no secrets in families—just things no one wants to talk about.

I write about the concept of "counting heads" most clearly in "Beautiful, Boring Days" because I believe that the best days of our lives are often the days when nothing special happens.

Some pieces have been edited slightly, and always with the intention of clarifying and improving my words. In some cases, I've caught errors that even my editors overlooked. While the pieces were written with specific people and incidents in mind, I hope their messages are also broad, so many readers can relate to my stories.

The section, ONE FAMILY'S BACK PAGES, contains stories about my search for family, which was motivated by the breakdown of ties due to separations, divorces, the Holocaust, and immigrations. Finding my second-cousin, Eva, and listening to her stories about war-time life in Hungary, was a life-changing experience for me. I wrote about her over a period of years; rather than eliminate some of the stories, sometimes, I have repeated small but important parts of her life, and my times with her.

Readers may notice that some thoughts and phrases appear (and reappear) in different pieces; mentioning that I was 2-years-old when my mother left my father and took my older brother and me to live with my grandmother are essential descriptions of who I am. In some ways, they even define who I am. Even when I myself don't realize it.

If, at times, I seem to be complaining about "parenthood," all in all, I loved it. Looking back, when I think about all those years I spent raising kids, I know I was lucky to have had that time with them. Ken worked full time, and I worked whenever I could. Weekdays, as soon as Edward and Peter left for school, I headed for my home office and worked and wrote until the boys came home.

I still get (and love getting) fan letters. Following is one of my essays, published in *Woman's Day* in 1986. Soon after, a fan from the mid-West wrote to me and praised it. Thirty years later, he wrote to me again, asking if I had any spare copies of "Gone Tomorrow, But Forever in our Hearts" because the original one, posted for years on his family's refrigerator door, had "worn out." I wrote back, saying I did; in fact, I had a few copies of the entire magazine, and sent one to him with my thanks for asking.

This piece begins on the following page.

GONE TOMORROW, BUT FOREVER IN OUR HEARTS

Is it better not to know when the last time something special—and yet ordinary—occurs? Should it slip away silently, when no one is looking?

My son's room has two occupants—a ghost and a teenage boy. I never see the ghost, but I sense his presence when he stirs the air gently, bringing back faint scents of baby powder and diaper cream, or when a late afternoon sunbeam strikes, for a moment, a once beloved Matchbox car. On the bulletin board above the teenager's desk tickets to a rock concert hide faded blue ribbons from a fourth-grade track meet. Where dolls (yes, dolls) once leaned lopsidedly on shelves, there are now disorderly piles of records, term paper notes, tape cassettes and drum sticks. *Tubby the Tuba* has been replaced by *Rolling Stone*.

The room has changed along with the child, and I am left remembering all the times we spent within it and wondering when the ordinary and regular activities of childhood suddenly stopped. When did those past times become last times?

It's not easy to see my younger child growing up. Peter is part of a very limited edition, only two boys, just two and a half years apart. When they were little, I always rushed the older one, encouraging him to be bold, take chances and do things on his own. Consequently, he often hung back and moved reluctantly into his future, keeping one eye squarely focused on his past—a position still occupied by his brother Peter, the one permitted to do things like a baby, the baby he still was.

Peter didn't hold back. He moved forward without hesitation, following in his brother's footsteps when it suited him and venturing out on his own whenever he chose. Being Number Two had advantages: No one expected him to move ahead until he was ready.

I enter Peter's room quietly, half believing that any loud noises or movements may upset the cockeyed balance of adolescent order. This is not the room I lovingly decorated when he was first born. The mural I painted of clapboard houses and tidy shops in a row on Main Street has been covered, like an ancient fresco, by layers of paint and baseball pennants. Also gone is the cherry-red carpeting, replaced by one in serious beige.

I remember sitting with Peter on the old red rug, our heads resting against the side of his bed. He has just had a bath, and small drops of water from his slickly combed hair drip onto the collar of pajamas covered with dancing bears. Peter chooses a book from a stack nearby, and we begin to read. The story moves along with predictable innocence. If good things break, they can be fixed; if bad things happen, they can be corrected or at least understood. Life makes sense in a children's book. As we turn the pages, we feel secure in our world and confident that things will remain the same.

Over the years, we read many stories. First, I read to him, as he snuggled in my arms or right next to me on the cushy pillows we laid on the floor. Then he began to "read" the story to me. When he actually learned to read, we would discover new books together, and Peter would identify words, sounding out those he did not know for sure.

As he grew older, I still read to him often, especially on long rainy days. Eventually, I read to him only when he was sick and needed to be treated like the little boy he once had been.

And then I read to him... not at all. I remember many times when I read to Peter, but not the last time.

Often, we rarely notice the last time we do something we have done hundreds of times before. One day we realize those times are over. The little boys who caught the ball we threw now play for the high school baseball team, and the little girls who asked us to sing them lullabies now sing for children younger than themselves.

Last times can occur only when there have been many times. Those once-in-a-childhood experiences—winning a contest, starring in the school play—are special and unforgettable. Yet when we look back, they're not as poignantly remembered as the day-to-day ordinary occurrences: tucking in a child and kissing him good night; untying the knots in small tattered shoelaces; squeezing sudsy water from a washcloth and watching it run down a child's smooth warm back. Why didn't I stop and notice?

Must last times come and go, empty of any ceremonial goodbyes?

When my sons were babies, the only times I thought about were all the "firsts" to come: first teeth; first words; first steps. And eventually, their first days of school. Days crept by during each boy's infancy, filled with the routine of baby care. Then, in a wink, milestones were reached, and with each new achievement, I anticipated more. Life seemed a series of new beginnings.

Looking back, I now realize there were endings too. We can't stop last times from happening, in parenthood or any other parts of life. Nor could we ever bear to know when a last time was occurring any more than we could bear knowing what is to come.

I no longer read stories to Peter, but sometimes he'll tell me about something he's just read. I don't care if he's describing a scene from *Hamlet* or an article in *Modern Drummer*. It's the moment itself that I appreciate. I realize it's what I've always enjoyed the most.

I want to ask him, "Do you remember?" and draw him into my fond recollections. But that would not be fair; I'm not looking for praise. Besides, the past is long ago to him— longer ago, I think, than it is to me.

Will he remember? Yes, I think someday he will. Ghostly breezes waken adolescent memories too. But while neither of us will recall every detail of a childhood now over, snippets of events will surface in our thoughts. When was the last time I...? When was the last time he...? Does it matter, as long as we remember how it felt?

Woman's Day — June 17, 1986

LOVE
AND
MARRIAGE

Susan J. and Ken Gordon

I MARRIED HIM

Reader, I married him.
So begins the final chapter of *Jane Eyre*, Charlotte Bronte's nineteenth-century novel about a penniless young governess with pluck and integrity who comes to the mysterious and haunting Thornfield Hall, and eventually marries Mr. Rochester, the master of the house. Parts of Jane's story are deeply distressing, but others are poignant and breathlessly romantic. Senior year, in my high school Honors English class, we read *Jane Eyre*, wrote essays on the themes, and debated the merits of marrying "only for love." I thought the concept was naive and unrealistic, and said so.

One morning, pink-and-white signs posted in the school hallways announced an upcoming "Sweethearts Dance." Soon, our utilitarian gymnasium would be converted into a springtime bower of pink, white, and red blossoms enhanced by colored lights. I'd never been invited to a dance; would someone ask me now?

The next day, one of my classmates, a handsome football player named Ken, approached me after English class. He wanted to talk about *Jane Eyre*. "You were kidding, weren't you, when you said you wouldn't marry for love?" he asked.

"I mean, I wouldn't marry *just* for love," I explained. "There has to be more—you both have to love the same things, or at least some of the same things. Otherwise, I don't think you can stay in love."

"Oh, OK," he said, nodding. "I understand, and I think you're right."

That evening, Ken called and asked me to the Sweethearts Dance. I paused, hoping to keep him on edge for at least thirty seconds. Then I said yes!

For the next three weeks, I daydreamed about my dress, the dancing, and Ken. But a few days before the big event, it was canceled because not enough students had signed up. I was crushed, but Ken and I went out that evening anyway. We saw each other a few more times before graduation, and went to different colleges the following fall. For a while, we kept in touch by telephone and mail, chatting primarily about our passions—literature and drama. I dated and fell in and out of love with at least a dozen other young men. Ken subsequently admitted that he'd had some amorous adventures, too. After several years, we lost touch, until we both were attending graduate schools in New York City.

I must tell you that I have always been touched by married couples who describe their courtships and wedding days as if they were truly remarkable events, instead of fairly ordinary occasions. What brought Ken and me back together was not something awesome or amazing, but simply the fortuitous timing of our birthdays, only six days apart. Ken sent me a sweet birthday card, letting me know he was currently in law school in Manhattan. Usually, his handwriting was difficult to read, but this time he had printed out his return address on the envelope very carefully and clearly.

Even when I was dating other men, I always knew that Ken had been the brightest, funniest, and most passionate young man in my life. Because of all these reasons, I am happy to say that I had the good sense that day to race to the corner stationery store, buy a birthday card, and immediately mail it to Ken. Within a year, dear reader, I also married him.

We still read, write, and talk about books like crazy. When our eldest son became engaged, we started thinking about weddings and famous couples in history. How did the film star Grace Kelly meet Monaco's Prince Rainier? Did the comedian Henny Youngman really mean it when he said, "Take my wife, *please!*"? And just how grand was Queen Victoria's wedding to her beloved Albert?

I began doing research on great marriages, and before long, I was hard at work on *Wedding Days: When & How Great Marriages Began*. Ken helped out often, on evenings and on weekends. I might have written the book without him, but I never could have accomplished it so well or so joyously.

We learned that not much has changed throughout the centuries. Brides and grooms have always had last-minute jitters, intermarriages have always taken place, and many parents still think that no one is good enough for their "perfect" child (even if that person is Marc Chagall or Irving Berlin).

Those parents who supported their son's or daughter's decisions about marriage were the ones with whom their children remained close. But parents who criticized their children's choices, or tried controlling them by withholding love or money, rarely succeeded in getting their way and usually lost touch with their children. Century after century, in the middle of all those melodramatic maelstroms, were young lovers bent on matrimony, proving again and again that love really does "conquer all."

First encounters were rarely remarkable. Future spouses met by chance or by introduction, in classrooms and offices, at lectures and dances, on ships, trains, and planes, or after catching sight of each other across proverbial "crowded rooms." George Washington met Martha Custis at a dinner party in Williamsburg, Virginia. Almost two hundred years later, another future president also met his first lady in a similar setting. "I leaned across the asparagus and asked her for a date," said John F. Kennedy, remembering when he first spoke to Jacqueline Bouvier in a Georgetown mansion.

Ken and I still have our favorite couples, whose endearing stories warm our hearts. Here's one: In 1644, the English statesman and writer Sir Richard Fanshawe married Anne Harrison in Oxford, England. After King Charles was beheaded in 1649, the Fanshawes sided with the Royalists until Sir Richard was captured by Oliver Cromwell's troops and imprisoned at Whitehall in 1651. Rain or shine, Anne stood beneath her husband's prison window every morning at 4am, which was the only time they could see each other for months, until she won his release. It rained a lot that year, and Anne later recalled how the rain fell in her collar and came out by her heels. Eventually, she wrote her memoirs about their life together. This is what she wrote about Richard, more than 350 years ago: "Glory be to God, we never had but one mind throughout our lives. Our souls were wrapped up in each other's, our aims and designs one, our loves one, and our resentments one. We so studied one the other, that we knew each other's mind by our looks. Whatever was real happiness, God gave it me in him."

Even today, you can't beat that.

Victoria — May/June 2009

WEDDING DAZED

As soon as I said, "Yes, I'll marry you," I panicked. Had I actually uttered those four bombshells?

Ken was ecstatic. I was trembling. Not that I didn't want to marry him, but now that I had said yes, things would happen. Plans would be made.

Already, Ken was compiling lists of people to call, reception sites to check out, and honeymoon locations to consider. He was contemplating names for our first-born child when I wailed, "Slow down!"

"Don't worry," he chirped. "Everything will be just fine. The main thing is we're getting married."

That's what Ken kept saying for the next six months, and that's what I recited every time I panicked. Choosing a ring, shopping for my gown, and hiring a caterer and band threw me into temporary tailspins, but I kept repeating Ken's mantra.

By the time I dropped the invitations into the mail, I felt like Alice in Wonderland tumbling down the rabbit hole. Things were beyond my control.

Much later, after the "*I dos,*" I was sorting through some biographies and found I was not the first spouse-to-be with jitters. Famous people had been affected too.

"I don't know why, but I am simply terrified of the wedding ceremony, wrote Anton Chekhov to his fiancee in 1901. If the world-famous Russian playwright was scared silly, why not me? He told Olga Knipper he'd marry her only if she swore to tell no one in advance. Mum's the word, said

Olga, but Anton fretted anyway, and arranged a luncheon for their friends held at the same time as the nuptials. By the time the guests figured out what had happened, the newlyweds were on their honeymoon.

"I wish the awful day was over," naturalist Charles Darwin wrote to Emma Wedgwood in 1839. She was amused by "Charley's" lists debating the virtues and vices of matrimony. Not marrying meant "freedom to go where one liked" and "not being forced to visit relatives," but marriage would bring love and "a constant companion." They celebrated afterward on a honeymoon train bound for London, and soon settled down to a lifelong, love-filled marriage.

"Got to thinking about Mina and came near to being run over by a streetcar," Thomas Edison wrote. The great inventor fell in love fast, but he wondered if he would survive the wedding. "I'm getting pretty scared," he told Mina, his bride-to-be. "I wonder if I will pull through. I know that you will, women have more nerve than men." If Edison believed that, he certainly didn't know me!

I could relate to Eleanor Roosevelt's anxieties as she prepared for her St. Patrick's Day wedding in New York City. "Try and forget the crowd and only think of Franklin," her aunt advised. She also told Eleanor to drink a cup of strong tea, "to give you color and make you feel well." Eleanor was a wreck because the St. Pat's marching bands and hundreds of noisy people were parading by their Fifth Avenue town house. The throngs of well-wishers almost prevented President Teddy Roosevelt—who was giving away the bride—from getting through the door!

I was a catatonic bundle of nerves throughout my engagement. What if the band forgot to show up? What if the guests hated the soup? And what if my love for Ken wouldn't last the lifetime stretching before us? Fortunately, he was the essence of calm.

Happily, two days before our wedding, I lapsed into a remarkably composed, tranquil condition. All the arrangements were in apple-pie (maybe I should say, wedding-cake) order.

I still celebrate my marriage to Ken, the man whom I continue to fall in love with every day, 33 years later. As the Scottish author Sir Walter Scott said when he married Charlotte Carpentier, "When care comes, we will laugh it away, or if the load is too heavy we will sit down and share it between us till it becomes almost as light as pleasure itself."

Every couple should be so lucky.

Brides — May/June 2000

WEDDING PEARLS

A handful of pearls—once part of my grandmother's necklace—were among my small, priceless possessions for many years. I was nineteen when Grandma died, and my aunt gave the necklace to me.

"She'd want you to have it," my aunt said. "After all, she always called you her 'One and Only.'" As the sole granddaughter among five grandsons, I was especially precious to Grandma. I knew that she adored me, and I adored her, too.

Now, tinged with the aching sadness of losing my beloved grandmother was the bittersweet joy of having her cherished pearls. They were classy and elegant, lustrous and sophisticated. As I held the strand in my hand, it seemed both weightless and weighty. I can't recall Grandma wearing any other jewelry.

The pearls were not individually knotted, so they clicked together softly whenever they were touched. The largest was at the center, with slightly smaller ones graduating in size all the way to the back. As fashions changed throughout the years, few women wore pearls in this style anymore.

Two years later, I wore the necklace on my wedding day. Of course, it was "something old," although this hadn't occurred to me until a bridesmaid pointed it out. I sat before a mirror as she secured the clasp at the back of my neck, and memories of the past rose up and merged into the present. The phrase *tears of joy* may be a cliché, but that's what I was feeling deep inside. Not only did the heirloom connect me with Grandma, it also linked me to my earlier life as a much-loved granddaughter with my future one as a loving wife.

I was glad that Grandma had met my husband-to-be, although none of us knew that I would marry him someday. Ken and I had dated briefly in high school and had been good friends for a long time. One year, during winter break from our respective colleges, he called to ask me out. Grandma was staying at my house, and she was pleased to know she would finally meet "that nice young man." In fact, she decided to change into something a little nicer, although her everyday clothes looked perfectly fine to me. (Did she sense that Ken would be my 'One and Only?')

When the doorbell rang at 7pm, she was wearing a lovely blue dress, polished navy shoes, and her pearls, and was sitting on the living room sofa. Ken came in and sat down beside her. They chatted for a few minutes while I returned to my bedroom to finish dressing. (To be honest, I was ready, but I wanted them to spend a few minutes together.) Later, he told me she was pleased to hear that he loved good literature, art, and music, because they mattered to her, too. "Then she patted my hand and told me to take good care of you," he said. "I imagine she just meant that night, but maybe she meant something more!"

On a festive evening, a few years after Ken and I were married, I wore Grandma's necklace when we went out for dinner. I can't recall if I touched the strand or not, but suddenly it broke. The pearls clattered to the floor and scattered swiftly in all directions, like unruly children. Waiters hurried to my side, and we got down on our hands and knees, scrambling to collect the pearls. Diners at nearby tables looked around, too, and scooped up a few more for me. Weeping, I wrapped the pearls in a handkerchief and put them in my purse. Later, I realized there were no longer enough for a necklace. I kept the remaining ones in a little silk pouch and stored them in a dresser drawer.

A generation later, I offered the pearls to my future daughter-in-law shortly before she married my son. Melissa was touched by their history and didn't mind that they had yellowed somewhat and weren't as white as her dress. "They're perfect for 'something old,'" she said. "But I'd wear them anyway, because they mean a lot to you."

The next time I saw the pearls was on Melissa's wedding day. As she held her father's arm and walked down the aisle, the glistening jewels caught the light. Near Melissa's wrists, stitched on with great care at the end of each sleeve, was a sweet swirl of Grandma's pearls.

Victoria — May/June 2015

IDA B. WELLS & FERDINAND BARNETT: BUILDING A LIFE

Behind every great man stands a woman, they say. But in the case of Ida B. Wells, it was Ferdinand Barnett, a turn-of-the-20th-century Black lawyer and journalist, who stood behind his wife. This outspoken woman was so brave she compiled and published a scathing history and statistical record of lynchings in post-Civil War America, lectured and wrote about civil rights injustices, and sued a Southern railroad for denying her a first class seat.

And this was before she married him.

Long before anyone was called a mover and a shaker, Wells was. She and Barnett were lifelong crusaders for equal rights for Blacks. While she could be blunt and serious, he was gentler and more sociable. In this union, Wells was always more famous and powerful, but Barnett was the enabler, giving unending support and tireless assistance.

He had been born free in Nashville, and studied law in Chicago. Shortly after graduation, he established the Conservator, the first Black newspaper in town. As a lawyer, Barnett often represented underdogs, defending those who had no one else to defend them, whether or not they could pay. His first wife died when he was in his mid-thirties, leaving him with two young sons and enough good humor and confidence to marry a strong-willed woman.

Wells was born to slave parents in Mississippi, right before the Emancipation Proclamation was issued. She grew up during the all-too-brief era of Reconstruction, when Blacks truly believed that equality of opportunity was theirs. But Reconstruction collapsed by the 1880s, and odious Jim Crow laws were enacted, curtailing liberties and indirectly sanctioning mob violence, arson, and lynchings of Blacks.

Wells taught school in Memphis, and edited the Free Speech newspaper. After eight years, she was fired from her teaching job for writing editorials condemning the second-rate education Black children received in the city. When three Black merchants were horribly murdered by a white man, her angry editorials brought national attention, and the Free Speech offices were torched and destroyed.

Barely thirty years old, Wells met Barnett in the early 1890s to discuss a lawsuit regarding libel. They also collaborated with Frederick Douglass and other Black leaders, and co-authored an 81-page pamphlet protesting the lack of Black representation in the 1893 World's Columbian Exposition, held in Chicago. Romance blossomed between the two activists, and when Wells turned down a speaking tour in England, she and Barnett were married.

The newlyweds took a three-day honeymoon and went right back to work. Wells bought the Conservator and became its editor, publisher, and business manager. Nothing fazed the bridegroom—even when his spouse announced she was keeping her own name.

Women's rights activist, Susan B. Anthony, strongly disapproved of the marriage, declaring it would distract

Wells from more significant matters. But Anthony underestimated Wells's determination; even the births of four children slowed her down only temporarily. She stayed home a great deal but continued to write about issues such as the dangers of mob rule, jobs for Black women, public school integration, and women's suffrage. Wells also established a kindergarten in a poor Black neighborhood. Barnett kept an "extended office" at home, organized Athletic Clubs for boys and girls, and became more politically active.

By the time the youngest Barnett was eight, Wells returned to public life full-time, with a husband who actually liked cooking dinner, and a housekeeping staff to handle everything else. Wells and Barnett were involved in many legal cases, including the defense of Black prizefighter, Jack Johnson, accused of kidnapping a white woman who became his wife.

Race riots and lynchings continued, even in the North. In 1909, a Black man was lynched in Cairo, Illinois, and Governor Charles Deneen suspended the local sheriff temporarily for not protecting the victim. Someone had to appeal to the governor on the dead man's behalf, but Barnett (now an assistant state's attorney) was bound by his office to stay out of it. He prepared a legal brief for Wells, who successfully convinced Deneen not to reinstate the sheriff because it would incite more lawlessness and violence. From that time on, there were no more lynchings in Illinois.

Until their deaths in the 1930s, Wells and Barnett fought against Black oppression and discrimination.

The 20th century has not seen an end to racism or civil injustices, and Wells's words still entreat us:

"With malice toward none, but with charity for all, let us undertake the work of making the "law of the land" effective and supreme upon every foot of American soil—a shield to the innocent; and to the guilty, punishment swift and sure."

The Philadelphia Inquirer — August 16, 1999

WILL & KATE'S WEDDING BELL BLUES

Hearty felicitations on your engagement, Kate and William! Most of your wedding decisions sound great, but your choice of the date has sent me reeling in shock.

Maybe you didn't know that April 29 was the day Adolf Hitler married Eva Braun in 1945. But surely, someone in the royal household might have checked. Sixty-five years earlier, that early morning ceremony in a Berlin bunker still sends shivers up and down many spines.

Fooling around with the Fates is always risky; can't you pick another day? Or, as my grandmother used to say to the fruit man when he offered her bruised bananas, "Is this the best you can do?"

Certainly, there are things even future sovereigns can't control, like awful weather or those dreaded last-minute cancellations after you've spent weeks determining who sits where and it's too late to get a refund from the caterer. But you should have no trouble finding a new date for your nuptials. When you strolled around Westminster Abbey, I wish you had thought about some of the great people who are interred and remembered there, and chosen one of their wedding days instead.

For starters, there were King Edward the Confessor and Edith Godwin, married on Jan. 23, 1045. Everyone was glad when Edward ascended to the throne, replacing that wretched Dane, Harthacanute, who had treated

England shabbily. Edith's father, the pushy Earl of Wessex, introduced her to the native-born monarch, who thought she was beautiful and bright, as well as suitably God-fearing. She thought Edward was affable and gentle, although a bit pale. Most of the time, their kingdom was at peace, and they devoted themselves to religion and early construction of Westminster Abbey.

June 11, 1594 was the wedding day of English poet Edmund Spenser and Elisabeth Boyle, and it was "the joyfulest day that ever sun did see," he said. She—not the Virgin Queen—inspired her remarkable husband, called "the Prince of Poets of His Tyme," to write some of the finest Elizabethan love poems. Describing his bride, he wrote, "Her goodly eyes like sapphires shining bright, her forehead ivory white. Her cheeks like apples which the sun hath rudded. Her lips like cherries charming men to bite."

Poet William Wordsworth married Mary Hutchinson on Oct. 4, 1802. "Oh, William," she wrote. "I cannot tell thee how I love thee, and thou must not desire it—but feel it. I feel it in the fullness of thy soul and believe that I am the happiest of wives." He replied, "I love thee so deeply and tenderly and constantly—that I scarcely can bring my pen to write of anything else." Much of Will's best work, including completion of "The Prelude," was written after his marriage to Mary. Eventually, he became poet laureate of England.

One of the world's most romantic love stories began on Sept 12, 1846, when 39-year-old Elizabeth Barrett slipped out of her father's London townhouse to marry the 33-year old poet and playwright, Robert Browning. The wedding ring was put on and quickly removed before the bride and groom left St. Marylebone Church by separate doors. One week later, they ran off to Italy, and Elizabeth escaped her tenacious father's grasp and home forever. As she later wrote in "Sonnets from the Portuguese," because of Robert, "the face of all the world has changed."

Will and Kate, if you are still determined to marry in April, how about when Elizabeth, the future Queen Mum, married Prince Albert in 1923? They were married in Westminster Abbey on the 26th. Elizabeth knew that marrying into the royal family meant a life governed by rules and restrictions and she expected to be only the Duchess of York. No one anticipated that "Bertie's" older brother, Edward, would renounce the throne to marry Wallis Simpson fourteen years later. And no one foresaw that Elizabeth's warmth, sincerity and strong sense of duty would help restore the monarch to public favor after that scandalous abdication. She would always be the favorite of her father-in-law, King George V. Years later, he recalled that April 26 "was rather gray and inclined to rain, but as soon as the bride arrived at the Abbey, the sun shone as it always does in her presence."

Los Angeles Times — December 1, 2010

LOVE *"SIN-CERE"*

Sometimes, the loveliest walks take place on country lanes made of dirt worn down over the years. Clay surfaces are best, because the surface yields gently beneath your feet, and the soft sounds of shoes treading on ground are soothing to the ears, as well as to the mind and body. And sometimes, the subtle yielding of the ground is like the yielding of partners in a lasting marriage.

Years ago, I took such a walk on a summer afternoon in a small town near Boston, when I was visiting my elderly aunt and uncle. They'd been married for more than fifty years, and they still were delighted to be together.

I was a young adult, no longer living in what was then called a "broken home," because my parents were divorced. Even so, the old aches and pains of a shattered childhood could depress me without warning. Not now, I told myself; I am spending today with an old-married couple—a couple who had figured out, long ago, how to live together.

Aunt Sel had prepared a simple lunch of tuna salad, tomatoes, fresh bread and iced tea, which we ate together on a table by a picture window. Bright white dishes rested on pale blue placemats, and sunlight shone through clear water goblets. In the center of the gleaming teakwood table was an earthenware bowl, one of the many pieces of pottery that Sel had made.

We talked about books, the Red Sox, and our family. My uncle Leo smiled broadly whenever Sel spoke, and she listened intently to his old stories as if they were new. The day was hot, but a small breeze drifted in an open window. Sel hadn't left the house for days, because Leo had been feeling poorly. But now he turned on the TV to watch a baseball game, and he encouraged us to take a walk.

Near their home was a well-trodden footpath bordered by white clapboard houses with wide front porches and flower gardens bursting with zinnias, marigolds, and ageratum in a happy hodgepodge of colors. Sel and I walked slowly, following the road and the contours of the land, and letting our conversation ramble as well.

She became a ceramist after they married, and made fabulously beautiful objects out of dull brown clay which she kneaded, twisted, thumped and pounded. After the clay was wedged and prepared, she would break off a hunk and center it on her potter's wheel, squeezing and guiding the shape right out of the clay. She made bowls, platters, vases, and planters. Each piece was well-shaped and useful, and glazed in earth-tones.

In some ways, Sel and Leo were not alike—he was a practical businessman, she was a day-dreaming artist often lost in thought; he was punctual, and she refused even to wear a watch—but they had always been keenly accepting of each other. Also, and unlike other (less contented) couples I knew, they didn't try to change each other. Sel always said what matters most—in art as well as life—is being honest and sincere.

Whenever Sel sat at her potter's wheel, she would straddle the table and grasp the clay with both hands. Although she seemed to surround the clay, it was the clay itself which determined what she made, not the other way around. Like a gardener tenderly pruning a small bush to help it grow, the way Sel handled her clay was how she brought the beauty out. She searched for the beauty within each lump of clay, and did not impose her designs upon it.

All of Sel's creations are products of the earth – clay baked in fiery hot kilns and glazed in the colors of nature. Whenever I hold them in my hands, I think about the word, "sincere," which dates back to ancient Rome (at least). Back then—it's been said—second-rate sculptors hid the defects in their work by filling in rough, uneven cracks and crevices with wax. Inexperienced buyers were often fooled until the first hot day, when the wax melted and the defects reappeared. Only the finest works were "sin-cere" – without wax. Nothing was hidden: what you saw was what you got. Like a plain dirt road, Sel and Leo's marriage, and Sel's pottery.

The baseball game was still on when we returned home. "I've missed you," my uncle told us, but I knew he really was speaking just to Sel. In many ways, she and Leo were an ordinary couple, but their long life together showed me that a straightforward acceptance of each other is an essential part of a good and love-filled marriage.

First published here, in <u>Counting Heads</u> — 2023

FAMILY MATTERS

Susan and older brother, Mike 1954

IN THE COMPANY OF THE PAST

In the photograph that hung on my bedroom wall when I was a child, it is 1912. My grandmother is wearing a honey-toned satin dress, edged in fine lace, and a strand of seed pearls around her neck. She is a slim, young woman with lustrous brown hair piled on top of her head. In her arms is her beautiful baby daughter, who is dressed in a long white cotton gown and wrapped in a soft fur throw.

I don't remember when I first noticed the photo. It had always been there, beside my bed. I saw it when I went to sleep at night and played beneath it during the day. When I look at it now, it's me I'm remembering, as a little girl.

My mother, brother, and I lived with my grandmother since I was two years old, when my parents separated. My mother went to work and my grandmother took care of us. Weekday mornings, she gave us our breakfasts, packed our lunches, and sent us off. When she kissed me goodbye, I smelled a sweet mixture of shampoo, soap, and her morning cup of coffee.

On rainy days and lazy winter afternoons, when I was home from school and particularly bored or restless, she'd take a break from housework and sit with me. As we sifted through the piles of family photographs, she would tell me stories. "This is your Aunt Sel, before she was married. She was going to art school. That's one of her paintings in the background." Or, "These are your parents, when they first met. They married so quickly…. And they were so young."

Some photographs were of my grandmother's parents, taken soon after they came to America. My sweet-faced great-grandfather sits on an ornate chair, and his solemn wife and young children stand right beside him. Everyone stares at the camera. Taking pictures had once been serious business; you put on your best clothes and went to a photographer. Years later, my brother and I still put on "dress-up" clothing, but everything took place outside. "Look toward the sun!" my mother would say, and consequently, in all my childhood pictures, I am squinting.

There are no photographs of the interior of our home. There is no picture of my grandmother cooking, ironing, reading the newspaper, or making dresses for me on her Singer sewing machine. Nor is there a picture of my mother's dressing table where she sat and transformed herself, before my eyes, from a pretty woman to a most beautiful one. And yet, I can see these people, and see the rooms they occupied, as clearly as if they were in pictures in an album. I see every piece of furniture, where everything stood, and how the sunlight shifted from our living room in the morning to the kitchen in the late afternoon. Photographs really aren't necessary when I think about home. Still, there are days when I am drawn to look at them.

Click! I am four-years-old, standing in front of a restaurant with my family. Since eating out was a treat, we probably were celebrating something, but I don't remember what. I do remember the green wool coat I am wearing and its deliciously soft velvet collar that I loved to press against my cheeks.

Click! My brother and I are shaking hands in front of our apartment house. We squabble all the time but my mother has asked us to assume a conciliatory pose. "You were happy together sometimes," she tells us. "Someday you'll want to remember this."

Click! I am dancing with a boy at a high school party. Since I'm the "new" girl in the neighborhood, for a short while I'm popular. Other teenage boys and girls dance more closely, with their hands around each other's necks. My partner and I smile and wave toward a friend, who catches our expressions with her new Polaroid camera. Caught in the photo is another boy, who is laughing in reaction to someone else's story. One day, this picture will be come especially dear to me, for it has unintentionally snapped the young man I will marry.

Click! I am holding Edward, my firstborn baby, in exactly the same way my grandmother held hers. I think about how much she loved me and know that I love my son as passionately and completely. My husband takes our picture, and then hangs the antique photo above the baby's crib; eventually, it will hang by his brother Peter's, too. It will be a part of their childhood years, as it once was a part of mine.

Today, my home is filled with photographs. It's my nature to save things—hold the moment and try to freeze it in a frame. Photos cover the kitchen wall: my sons win prizes, hit baseballs, wear costumes, sing camp songs, graduate from kindergarten, graduate from high school. Edward's blue eyes sparkle like his mother's, when I was a girl. Peter's smile resembles that on his great-great-grandfather's face. Who will look at these pictures in future years? Will a young child take them out of boxes some day and study them with fresh curiosity? Will our photographs explain what we were really like, or simply acknowledge that for a time, we were here?

Not long ago, I saw Edward in his room, looking through piles of family pictures. I started to approach but silently backed away. It had been a long time since he had shown any interest in the pictures, but now he was ready to leave for college. He handled everything with a gentle reverence and smiled to himself again and again.

I didn't need to take a photo of Edward that day, because the picture in my heart will last forever.

Victoria — January/February 1994

MAY YOUR LIFE BE ONE SWEET SONG

I keep my grandmother's autograph album on a shelf near my desk. When I hold it in my hands, I imagine her exchanging this velvet-bound book with other 13-year-old girls many years ago, and writing "forget-me-not" on the corners of its gold-edged pages—the wishes, hopes, and dreams they had felt for each other as well as for themselves.

"To Esther," wrote Clara. "Long may your life be, in happiness and in everlasting joy." "Live—not only exist," declared Biance. And Anna, another classmate, said, "May each minute, each hour of your life be a golden holiday."

The album is small but almost regal in its richness. The pages are thick, although they crumble at the edges now, and most of them have pulled away from the binding. To a young girl growing up on the Lower East Side of New York City, this book was probably a treasured possession. I often wonder what prompted my grandmother to save this album through years of marriage, the births and raising of children, years alone, and then the ten years she spent taking care of my brother and me.

When I was a child, I loved to look through this book. I knew it was special, even before I could read the words, because it made me realize that once, a very long time ago, my grandmother—that white-haired lady who loved me so, whose hands were toughened and yet soft at the same time, whose arms and legs ached with arthritis, whose eyebrows could be raised imperiously when something irked her or someone disregarded her instructions—had once been as young as I, dreaming about the future, and wondering what it would hold.

I would imagine Esther and her friends purchasing their albums in neighborhood stationery stores. Graduation time was coming, and the girls eagerly recorded their names and brief philosophies of life in each other's books. Wishes for romance and love were counterbalanced with images of independence:

You may fall from a tree-top
  You may fall from above,
But the greatest fall you'll ever have
Is when you fall in love.
- Beatrice

The albums were also brought to school, where teachers added their comments, using the opportunity to praise these budding individuals and spur them to heights unknown. "I trust your success here may be a stepping-stone to successes in your future," noted one. Another quoted Shakespeare, reminding my grandmother, "This above all, to thine own self be true. Thou canst not then be false to any man."

Did some of those writers sense that the albums would be permanent, that their words would be read in the far-off future? Perhaps that's why classmate Dora wrote, "In memory's casket, drop one pearl for me," and Joanna said,

Remember me when you are happy,
Keep for me one little spot,
In the depth of thine affection,
Plant a sweet forget-me-not.

After that brief season in the sunlight of school graduation, the albums were placed on shelves or tucked into drawers where they remained until the owners crossed other thresholds of life. Within eight years, my grandmother married and moved away, and she took the album with her. She married a man who owned his own business and his own horse and carriage! Within ten years, he switched to motor cars, they had three daughters, and they moved to Manhattan's Upper West Side. But the Depression of the 1930s brought hard financial times. The three daughters married, and my grandmother moved to a much smaller apartment. Her life was probably pretty quiet for a while until my parents divorced and my mother came to Grandma's, bringing my brother and me with her. She found a job, and my grandmother took care of us.

Fortunately, she was the kind of parent a child could live with. In cramped quarters, she never made us feel restricted. Did I want to paint? She set up the bridge table for me, right in the middle of the living room. Did I need to be alone for a while? No place was off-limits. She was exuberant and energetic, tackling the challenges of caring for us with optimism and confidence. She cooked, she cleaned, did the laundry, the baking, and the sewing. She quizzed us on our lessons and insisted we do well in school. Whatever dreams she might have had for herself at that time, she put aside. But maybe we were always part of her dreams. And maybe the best thing she could have wished for was the chance to raise children again.

That's why "granddaughter" is to me one of the sweetest words in the English language. It means to be loved by someone unconditionally. Even the sound of the word evokes splendor: GRAND daughter.

Today, memories of my grandmother are part of my children's lives. She's with me when I read to my children, sing to my children, and teach them how to bake and sew. She's near us when we're all together, laughing about some silly joke or story. And she's near me when I'm all alone, wishing I could help a small child who is unhappy, and wondering what I've done to make him feel that way. "As long as you love your children, and make sure they know it, everything will work out," I hear her saying. "Love—and family—are the most important things."

Now, it's another school year, and Edward, my 8-year-old son, has purchased his first autograph album. This event required a visit to three nearby stationery stores until a cream-colored leatherette album was selected. The pages are edged in gold.

"Would you sign my album?" he asks me when we get home. "You'll be the first one."

"I'd be honored," I tell him, and we sit down together at the kitchen table. I look at Edward and wonder, what can I write? Big thoughts swim through my head, and little ones surface, too. He is my firstborn child, named after my grandmother Esther. I remember how he looked last Halloween, and how he sings when he gets dressed in the morning. I remember how he walks slowly on his way to school, and then races home each afternoon. Will he save his book for a long, long time? And one day, will his child read it too?

What do I wish for him, what do I hope his life will be?

"May your life be one sweet song," I write, stealing this prayer from "Augusta," who wrote to his great-grandmother back in 1903.

"I like it!" Edward exclaims. And as I watch him walk away, I am sure I can hear him humming.

Victoria — September 1991

MY FATHER, MY FRIEND

The first time I met, him, he was just "Mr. Cohan" to me. One Saturday afternoon, my mother insisted I wash my face and hands, and get dressed up so I could escort her out of our apartment house and meet some man waiting by his car. She'd gone out with men before; what was different about this one? Why did I have to stop what I was doing and change my clothes for him?

Why? Because he had asked her to marry him the night before, I later learned. He had already met my brother. Now he wanted to meet me. "Hello, Mr. Cohan," I said, anxious to run back inside and return to my games. "Hello, Susan," answered a curly-haired, middle-aged man. He spoke softly, almost shyly, as he took my hand and shook it.

After he and my mother married, I didn't know what to call him, and for a long time, I didn't call him anything. My friend called her new stepfather "Uncle," but that seemed phony to me. "Leo" didn't seem right, either. He called me Susan, or Sue, as my mother and brother did. He didn't have to call me "Daughter:" did I have to say "Dad?" Who was this man to me? He seemed kind and gentle, and he even liked to have me around. But a father? Would calling him "Father" make him a father?

Stepping into a family already containing a mother, a teenage boy and an 11-year-old girl, Leo knew he wouldn't be treated like a father automatically. We were a long-established group; he was a new piece to be fitted in. It's not that he had to compete with any love we felt for our "real" father, a cold, self-concerned man who'd been anything but kind, anything but caring in all the years we had known him. Leo's job was harder—he had to compete with a fantasy, our unrealistically high expectations of what a perfect father should be: loving, caring, available, supportive, generous, clever and handsome. And, most of all, a perfect father would think his children were perfect, too.

He probably had his own fantasies. Orphaned as a young child, Leo had been raised by older brothers and sisters who, although they loved him, never put his interests first in their lives, the way a devoted parent would. His own first marriage had been sad and unsatisfying. Now, at the age of 50, he had married a woman with two children, accepting all the responsibilities and financial obligations that would entail.

That first year the four of us lived together, Leo spent a lot of time fixing and building things in our new home. It was his way of putting down roots, I guess, of establishing a firm foundation on which our new family could stand. He stained the wood paneling in the den, hung wallpaper in the bathrooms, and designed and constructed cedar closets in the basement. But at the same time we were becoming a family, I was becoming an adolescent. My mother and I, who had always been close, now seemed to argue all the time. "Why can't you behave?" she angrily asked me. "You won't let me do anything my way!" I countered, and stormed out of the room. I had to talk to someone.

I found Leo in the basement, working on the closets. Slowly, methodically, he was planing a piece of wood. Then he sanded it carefully, letting me talk, offering me a piece of sandpaper to help him smooth the edges, giving me a few nails to hold while he positioned the wood on the wall, and having me help him hammer it into place. "She's impossible!" I told him. "She yells at me for every little thing. Whatever I do has to be perfect to satisfy her."

He nodded as I talked, and kept on working. I wished he would take my side—how could anyone not?—but he knew he was caught in the middle. "Your mother only wants you to aim for perfection," he said softly. "That shouldn't be too difficult for you. I think you're pretty exceptional."

Leo and I spent a lot of time together in the basement that first winter. He taught me how to work with tools so I could build, paint, and repair things. That "shop" time became a good outlet for a lot of adolescent frustrations. That basement—which my mother rarely visited—became a "safe haven" for me to escape to. Leo was there for me whenever I needed him. He didn't solve my problems, but encouraged me to sort things out for myself. What I needed—and what he gave me—was a sympathetic ear. "You know," he once remarked, "you and your mother have a lot in common. You're both energetic, spirited, and strong-opinioned people. That's why you sometimes irritate each other. But that's what I like about you... the two of you."

Leo was a calm man, slow moving and contemplative. He loved to fish, but what appealed to him more than the desire to catch anything was the peacefulness and serenity he'd find on a lake in a rowboat. In fact, when he did catch something, he'd always chuckle, surprised that his "two-bits" lure actually worked. Then he'd hold the struggling fish gently in his hand, being careful not to squeeze too hard. Very quickly, he would slip the hook out of the fish's cheek, wipe its mouth with a rag the way a parent pats a child, and toss it back into the water. I'd never seen a fisherman so concerned about his fish.

Dinnertimes, he often brought home small, inexpensive surprises—a flowered light-switch plate for my bedroom wall, a sports magazine for my brother. Conversations at the table were lively. He listened to our stories about school, complaints about homework, tales about victories on the athletic field, and all our silly jokes. He always assumed we were smart and treated us as if we were. "Try this," he'd begin, and we knew what was coming—a new mind teaser he'd just heard at work, or read in the paper. He'd laugh in the end after we had figured out the answer. "I knew I couldn't trick you!" he'd boast, shaking his head but beaming at the same time.

The first June I lived with Leo, I biked to a popular men's store in town, with two weeks' allowance and all my baby-sitting money from the past month. Heady masculine aromas from after-shave lotions and colognes intoxicated me as I entered the store. I had never been in a men's shop before. Pictures of hunting scenes were mounted on dark wood-paneled walls, and rich plaid carpeting covered the aisle floors. Men's suits, ties, bathrobes, pajamas, shoes, slippers, and jewelry were displayed everywhere. At the age of thirteen, I had come to purchase my first Father's Day gift.

Maleness was no longer something to shy away from. Now I knew a man who was gentle and loving. Father's Day was not just for other families. This year it would be our holiday, too.

I selected a blue silk tie decorated with rows of tiny fish, and carried it home proudly. The next Sunday morning, I gave it to Leo, who put it on immediately, right over his pajamas. "Thanks so much," he said. "I'll treasure this." He put his arms around me and kissed my cheeks.

"You're welcome," I answered. "Happy Father's Day, Dad." I said it as casually as possible, but I saw him smile and knew he had heard me.

You might think that, because my natural father had been so cruel, I'd have welcomed any other man who was halfway decent. But memories of my childhood practically destroyed any hopes I had of having a warm, loving relationship with someone who tried to be a father to me. Before Leo came into my life, I'd had it with fathers. It was the simplicity, honesty and constancy of his friendship that won me, and I have never forgotten how lucky I have been.

Gradually, over time, our new family has created its own common roots and traditions. It was Leo who sent my brother and me to college, saw us married, and has now shared much of his time and love with our children—his grandchildren. Sure, they've been told he's a "step"-grandfather, but what's it to them? "Pa" has loved them since the days they were born. He took them for strolls in their carriages, read to them, and rocked them. Later on, he taught them how to fish and work with tools. He's been a one-man cheering squad at their soccer games, baseball games, piano recitals and school plays. Just as he used to do with me. Just as he taught me to do with my kids.

Children, I have learned, are entitled to be cared for by kind, loving adults who are not only parents to them but friends as well.

Leo chose my mother, and he chose my brother and me, too. We are family and friends by choice—not by birth or blood. His friendship—and his love—have been gifts that I will never forget.

McCall's — June 1985

WHO BELONGS ON THE FAMILY TREE TODAY?

When my 10-year-old son, Edward's class began working on family trees, the children were encouraged to ask their parents for help. "That's good, " I thought, taking a long, deep breath. I'd always figured that one day, either Edward or his younger brother Peter would be given this assignment, and I'd wondered how I would handle it. Family trees today can be forests of trouble.

It's not that I was worried about the research to be done. My family always liked looking through old photo albums and talking about relatives who had lived long ago. In fact, our family's "ancient history" is a snap, compared to what happened in recent years. We have step-grandparents, "real" grandparents, my husband's much younger half-sister (our sons' half-aunt?), a long-term loving relationship not "sanctified" by marriage, and two adopted cousins.

Currently, about a quarter of American children under the age of eighteen live only with their mothers, fathers, and siblings from that marriage. Defining "family" can be tricky. How do we decide whom to include or omit when drawing our family trees?

Both my husband and I grew up in families of divorce, so maybe that's why we've always been sensitive to these issues. When I was a kid, I wished I belonged to one of those old-fashioned groups—people whose ties go back generations, a clean line of forebears standing shoulder to shoulder throughout the years, with no shoots cut off prematurely, no divorces splintering key branches, and no boughs left hanging. The kind of family that would make you feel you really had roots. But nowadays, many families have "off-shoots" on their family trees, and having divorced parents is, unfortunately, a common reality.

After school one rainy afternoon, Edward sat at our kitchen table and began writing down the names of everyone in our family.

"Is it okay to write Pa's name for my grandfather?" Edward asked me. He was referring to his step-grandfather who had loved him from the day he was born. "Or am I supposed to write... your "real" father? And what about Aunt Barbara? Does she count, even if she and Uncle Jeff aren't married? I know that my cousins are mine even though they are adopted, but...." He sighed heavily and rested one hand against his cheek.

I hugged Edward and sat down beside him. Using an assortment of bright markers, he had decorated the borders of his family tree paper with elaborately curled vines and brightly colored autumn leaves. I knew that this assignment meant a lot to my son, because it would help him make sense out of things. But it also made me uncomfortable because it was forcing him to pigeonhole people and question their roles in our family—something that he'd never done before.

Edward never knew my father, who dropped out of my life when I was a teenager. But Pa taught Edward how to fish and play the drums. They took long walks together and shared silly jokes. Did my father belong on my son's family tree, or did that treasured place belong to my stepfather instead? And what about Aunt Barbara, who had lived with Uncle Jeff for many years? She never forgot Edward's birthday and loved spending time with him.

"Tell me—what do the words, 'family tree,' mean to you? I asked him.

He hesitated. "I'm not sure," he said.

"Then, what about the word, 'tree?' What's your idea of a really great tree?"

That was easier. A perfect tree was "leafy and green, big and strong," Edward said. "You could sit underneath it and feel it was protecting you."

"You're right," I told him. Then, I pointed to a large maple tree in our backyard, and said it was planted long ago by the first family to live in our house. "Once, it was a tiny sapling, and now it's even taller than our house. In the summer, it shades us and in the winter, sunlight streams through the bare branches and warms our house. But the branches are always there, summer and winter. The tree would die if it didn't have supportive branches."

"So what do you think about your family tree? I asked him. "After all, you're the person making it."

"I need to make two trees," Edward concluded. One would be the "official" version, and the other would contain the names of everyone who cared about him.

Who belongs on our family tree? In our case, it's all the people who make our family a family.

Long Island Parenting News — December 2001

GIVING THANKS

Framed photographs of six generations of people in my family grace my dining room wall. The oldest pictures are sepia-toned images of stalwart fathers sitting on stiff chairs, with their proud, unflinching wives standing by their sides. Their children are arranged right and left, holding hands or with their arms around each other. These are the immigrants who embarked on hazardous ocean voyages to come to America in the late nineteenth century.

Soon after the newcomers arrived, they put on their best clothes, went to a photographer's studio, and posed for pictures to send "back home." Being well-dressed meant you were succeeding financially, whether or not it was true. This was meant to comfort relatives in the "old country," and sometimes inspire them to come to America, too.

The pictures are always on display, but I never look at them as intently as I do before Thanksgiving Day. It's become a small ritual for me to have silent conversations with my ancestors as I set the table for my favorite holiday. I thank them for enduring the hardships of breaking away from everything they had ever known. Surely, it took great courage to say goodbye even to hardscrabble lives and few prospects of a better future. But, I always add, it was worth it.

About one hundred years ago, my grandfather, Aaron, boarded a ship in the port city of Antwerp and sailed to Ellis Island in New York. He traveled in summer, which was fortunate because the crossing took ten days and steerage, where he slept, was malodorous, dank and overcrowded. On warm days, at least he could stand on an open deck, breathe fresh air and see the sky.

Aaron wasn't the eldest child in his family, but he was the one with gumption and ambition. According to genealogical records that I've found, Aaron was 14, 17, or 19-years-old at that time, depending on who asked him. He had either no money or a few dollars in his pocket, also depending on who asked him. Back then, you wrote your story as you went along. Being young and strong helped you gain admittance to America; having some money helped too, even if you exaggerated a little.

Six years earlier, my grandmother, Etta, was 5-years-old when her mother led her and her three brothers off the barge that transported them from Ellis Island to lower Manhattan and into the waiting arms of Isaac, her husband and their father. Amid the raucous cacophony of ship engines, onshore machinery and incomprehensible languages, surely they would have recognized "Papa's" voice.

Turn-of-the-last-century photographers such as Louis Hine and Edward Steichen captured images of cheering and crying immigrants crowding the decks of ships pulling into New York harbor. I like to think that my relatives are somewhere in those pictures. Etta might be clutching a rag doll for comfort, as she searches for her father's face among the waving multitude. Aaron might be gripping a handrail or walking down a gangplank, and wondering if he had made the right decision to come to this exciting but somewhat bewildering place.

Even today, when you visit Ellis Island, you can sense the weighty importance of those powerful years in our nation's history, especially if you separate from tours and wander around the grounds by yourself. It's the stillness that speaks most loudly to me, and the absence of hullabaloo that swirled here for decades. Echoes of the past, and faint whispers of the millions of people who passed through the gates, resonate profoundly in the un-restored buildings and empty halls.

At Thanksgiving, it's become a tradition for someone in my family to read a favorite poem or quotation which reflects our feelings about being together. This year, with heartfelt gratitude for our good fortune, I'll be reading the words of the Nobel Prize winner, Albert Einstein, who fled Germany in 1933 for the safe haven of the United States of America:

"Strange is our situation here upon earth. Each of us comes for a short visit, not knowing why, yet sometimes seeming to divine a purpose. From the standpoint of daily life, however, there is one thing we do know: that we are here for the sake of each other, above all, for those upon whose smile and well-being our own happiness depends, and also for the countless unknown souls with whose fate we are connected by a bond of sympathy."

Victoria — November/December 2009

FINDING OURSELVES IN FAMILY PHOTOGRAPHS

It's easy to "photo-shop" people out of pictures these days, but as any genealogist will tell you, sending relatives to the "re-cycle bin" is usually a very bad idea.

Even before I became an amateur genealogist, I was the person in my family who saved our photographs and placed them in albums. My collection dates back to 1895, soon after my great-grandparents arrived in New York. Within weeks, they put on their best clothes and posed for pictures to send back home.

After my grandmother left my grandfather, Aaron, in 1938, she snipped his image out of all their photographs. Years later, my mother didn't bother to get rid of snapshots of my father when she got rid of him; she simply tossed them into the back of a closet. Those pictures, which survived years of indifference and neglect, have caused me to recognize my blue eyes and dimples in his face, too.

I had seen Aaron briefly, when I was very young, and faintly recall him as a stooped old man with wispy gray hair. But I had no idea how he looked when he was a well-to-do husband and father. All I had was part of one tattered picture, in which my then 3-year-old aunt is holding a man's left hand. That, and the tip of one well-polished shoe, is all you can see of Aaron.

Photographs are taken in less than a minute, but their impact outlasts lifetimes. Most families today have countless pictures of their children, but in the late 19th century, it was a new reality. As the late Susan Sontag said, "Never before in human history did people have any idea what they looked like as children…. to be able to see oneself and one's parents as children is an experience unique to our time."

Few children really see their parents when they are young and good-looking. In healthy families, parents and children remain close throughout their lives. Little by little, the children observe their parents' gradual deterioration as their health declines and youthful looks fade. Often, many years pass before adult children examine their parents' childhood and wedding pictures to search for hints of the present in those youthful faces and ask curiously, were these people really my mother and father long ago?

You have to know what family members look (and looked) like, to notice their features in the younger generation. It doesn't matter if a characteristic is desirable or not; what matters most is the satisfying confirmation of a family connection. "That's Uncle Leo's nose!" we assert, and "Grandma's wavy hair!" Personality traits can also span generations. "He's as stingy as my father's brother," or "Look at how she dances, just like her namesake."

I'd heard that Aaron had returned to Europe twice in the 1920s, to bring his widowed father to America. Wouldn't Aaron have needed a passport? When I learned that photographs were required beginning in 1914, I jumped at the chance to have copies of his pictures. Immediately, I filed requests with NARA (National Archives and Records Administration) to obtain the application numbers for Aaron's passports (he'd applied for at least two) and their storage file locations. Next, I hired an archives-approved vendor to photograph the pictures, which arrived a few weeks later.

In them, Aaron is vigorous and alert, nattily dressed, with a watch chain across his chest, and *pince-nez* on his nose. He is assertive-looking, well fed and strong, not humbled as he appeared in later years. He is a prosperous entrepreneur with a wife and three children. He is on his way up.

There are images we decide to keep, and those we choose to lose. But maybe it's best to keep every one, especially if your family's been shattered by breakups. I've always known I have my grandmother's nose, my mother's curls, and my great uncle Charlie's artistic abilities. Only after I obtained Aaron's passport photos did I consider that his appearance might be noticeable in his descendants. Now I see that he bears a strong physical resemblance to one of my cousins, also a very determined and successful businessman, and one of the grandsons whom Aaron never knew.

The Jewish Week of New York — July 16, 2010

TENDER BUTTONS, TENDER MEMORIES

Buttons clutter up the bottom of my sewing box. I fish inside, looking for pins or a spool of thread, and my fingers sift through old buttons, reminding me of what I used to wear. There are white pearl buttons from an angora sweater, and black beaded buttons from an evening dress. Alongside these are heart-shaped ones—jelly-red, shiny, and dime-store cheap. Pieces of our past are everywhere, even in the bottom of a box.

My Grandma Etta saved buttons in a round metal Louis Sherry candy tin, with a spray of violets painted on the lid. Whenever I complained that I had nothing to do, she suggested that I play with the buttons. So I counted, sorted, and arranged them in piles. It was satisfying work for a restless child trying to make sense of a troubled family life. But many years would pass before I appreciated the true value of the buttons. They would teach me the importance of seemingly trivial possessions, and affirm how much my grandmother loved me.

After my parents' divorce, my mother found a full-time job and my grandmother took care of us when we moved into her home. Before out-grown, castoff clothing was reluctantly discarded, she snipped off the buttons and put them in the candy tin. And sometimes, she made special outfits for me, like the ones we admired in elegant children's shops downtown.

"Which one do you like best?" she would ask, as we browsed through rich collections of finery. Once, I chose an exquisite pink dress with lace-edged sleeves; another time a dark wool plaid jumper with velvet trim. After praising my taste, she'd examine my selection to see how it was made. "Thanks, we'll think it over," she'd tell the saleswoman politely, as we left the store.

Next, we'd stop at a fabrics store, to search through bolts of polished cottons, tissue-thin silks, radiant velvets and soft woven wools until we found the perfect material for my dress. I stood before a mirror as my grandmother draped the fabric over my shoulder like a Roman toga. "Ahh!" she'd proclaim – it brought out the blue in my eyes, the rose in my cheeks, it brightened my smile and highlighted my hair. When we got home, she cut the fabric, pinned it, and began stitching it on her black and gold Singer sewing machine.

Shortly before Valentine's Day, we were browsing in a trimmings store, where a set of six red heart-shaped buttons caught my eye. Smooth and bright, like cherry candies, they were attached to a white card by a thread that broke when I touched it. Suddenly, the buttons slid off and bounced across the wooden floor. My grandmother and I got down on our knees and searched assiduously, but only three buttons could be found.

"It's a broken set now. Nobody will buy them," said the cashier, glaring at me.

"I will," said my grandmother, opening her purse.

"But they aren't useful," I whispered. She had taught me that jackets needed five buttons, shirts even more. "Three aren't enough to sew on anything."

"We'll see," she said, as she paid the cashier. "I suppose they'll be good for something."

For weeks, I kept the red heart buttons in my pocket and carried them around like good luck charms. My grandmother never complained about the cost, and eventually, I forgot about them. Yet here they were, buried in my sewing box. These buttons were never useful, in a practical way. They were good for nothing ... but good enough to keep. "Tender buttons," I think, recalling poet Gertrude Stein's apt phrase. Like valentines sent from another time and place, they still convey my grandmother's love for me. She was the one who stroked my hair and told me things would get better whenever they were bad. She defended me against that insensitive cashier, and shielded me from other hurts on countless occasions.

Now, as I hold the slick little buttons in my hand, they click together softly, bringing back faint memories of lazy afternoons and dark winter nights, soft melodies on the radio and bathtubs filled with hot steamy water, clocks that ticked and telephones we used to dial. Once again, I am sitting on my grandmother's rug, spilling buttons out of a round metal tin. She sits nearby, at her sewing machine. If I close my eyes, I can hear it humming, and listen to the sweet sounds of her voice as she describes what will become the most beautiful dress she ever made, for the most wonderful granddaughter anyone ever had.

Victoria — January/February 2009

MY STEPFATHER, MY FRIEND

For years after Leo died, people said to me, "I never knew he was your stepfather." You see, I never called him that. At first, he was no one special in my life. Then he became my friend. In time, he was my father too.

Leo married my mother when I was eleven; two years later we moved into a house in a new suburban development. At first, our lawn was just a mud pile with a few scraggly clumps of grass, but Leo saw bright possibilities. "Your mother wants flowers; she can plant them here, where there's lots of sun," he said. "We'll plant trees over there, to give us some shade. And in the backyard, I'd like a barbecue." Then he smiled. "After so many years of apartment living, now we can have cookouts!"

For years, Leo had lived in an apartment by himself, and now he was putting down roots in the suburbs. At first, our split-level house resembled all the others, but then it began to change. Little touches—my mother's flower garden, and Leo's trees—made our house unique. More important, a real family was forming within this house, with its own special traditions. Leo was becoming a full-time parent, and I was learning what it meant to have a father.

Weekday mornings when the weather was bad, Leo often drove me to school. Having a father drop you off may have been something my classmates took for granted, but

I always thought it was wonderful. Saturday mornings, we went to the hardware store, then browsed in the five-and-ten, buying a sports magazine for my brother and something for me. Later, during dinner, Leo would tell us stories about his job and we'd talk about our friendships and schoolwork. "If you need any help, just ask me," he would say. "But I doubt that you need it. You two are awfully smart."

Some people might think that doing errands and eating meals together are nothing special, but I, who had previously spent my childhood watching other families do these everyday activities, savored them with intense delight. Looking back, I realize that Leo gave me what I needed most—the experience of doing ordinary things together as a family.

One day, we learned that my "real" father—who hadn't seen or supported my brother or me for more than five years—wanted to see us again, on a regular basis. We remembered too well the early years we had spent with him. He had been angry and cruel, violent and unloving. Since my brother was now 17-years-old, he didn't have to follow family court stipulations. But because I was still a "minor," I had to meet with a judge.

When Leo, my mother, and I entered the courtroom, my "real" father was already present. I avoided his glance and told the judge that now I was part of a new family, and that Leo taught me how to make things, took me to the movies, and helped me with my homework. I explained that he always listened to me and never raised his voice. I said I didn't want to see my "real" father because he had never shown any love for me, or even much attention.

The judge looked at Leo, and asked, "How are things going?"

"They couldn't be better," Leo answered. "I'm a lucky man to have such a family."

Aren't the best parents also friends to their children, accepting them without reservation and telling them they can be counted on? Stepfamilies aren't bound by traditional ties, so the love and friendship they develop is extremely precious. Was Leo "perfect?" He'd deny it if I said so. And that's one reason why he was so "perfect" to me.

Sometimes, during the first years that my new family lived together, I'd look out my bedroom window on warm summer nights and see Leo and my mother walking together in front of our house. My parents, I would think. I actually have two parents.

Soon after we moved to the suburbs, one of our new neighbors introduced herself to me. She had already met my mother and Leo. "You know," she remarked, "You look just like your father."

I knew she was just making conversation—but even so.

"Thank you," I said. Why tell her anything different?

Good Housekeeping — June 1993

TRIBUTE TO A MANUFACTURER'S REP SUGGESTS TRAITS OF SUCCESS

No one can teach you the secrets of marketing and salesmanship better than a successful salesman. And one of the best furniture salesmen, in the eyes of many New York area retailers, was my father, Leo J. Cohan, a manufacturer's representative for over 50 years.

Forget, for a moment, sales charts, consumer trends, discounts on bulk orders, and industry forecasts. Being a successful salesman doesn't just mean knowing how to "read" the market. It also means being an optimist, approaching each possible sale with an air of confidence, a sense of anticipation that this time, I'll write up a really terrific order.

While the commission of most representatives' lines is fairly constant, it's that unknown factor of "just how much business can I bring in this season?" that keeps a salesman motivated to try harder and sell more.

Yes, there are salesmen who are blustery, loud, slap-on-the-back people, who pump their customers' arms vigorously and think they're bowling 'em over with a persuasive personality and a can't miss collection of goods. They dish out the hard sell and the soft soap, and many make a good living doing it. But they'll rarely earn the respect, admiration, and long-term loyalty that my father won in his quiet, understated way.

Leo Cohan never made a sale by being pushy or overly aggressive. Rather, he promoted his sense of pride in his product, pointing out the beautiful workmanship and attention to detail. He also was generous with his time. If a store owner didn't understand complicated shipping schedules or a new price scale, Dad would sit down and patiently explain it.

A lady customer in Brooklyn said her table leg was wobbly; Dad came to repair it the next day. The button just popped on a leather sofa in Rye; he fixed it with his mending kit before the week was out. He never hesitated to drive long distances to check on a small complaint, saying that keeping his customers happy was as important as getting a new order.

Keeping himself happy was never hard to accomplish. Although selling furniture was Dad's favorite life-long pastime, he also loved to go fishing. He enjoyed it in many ways—on a party boat off the Florida coast, sitting in a small rowboat on a peaceful New England lake, or simply standing on the edge of a dock out in Montauk. It was the slow, repetitive act that attracted him—size up each situation carefully, determine the best bait to use, cast out your line with optimism and hope… and wait.

Fishing—like selling—required patience, persistence, and a bit of the gambler's passion. Each time Dad threw out his line or entered a customer's store, there was a new chance for making the biggest "catch" ever. Sometimes, he caught a fish, or made a sale, and sometimes, he didn't. But he never tired of trying.

If he didn't get a "bite," he headed for another part of the water—or his retail territory—with fresh expectations and an eagerness to try again. It was a never-ending game for him, and he considered himself lucky to work at a profession he loved.

In his last years, Dad was most content fishing on lakes or from the lawn of a lakeside summer house. (Preferably, at least one grandchild would be sitting beside him.) Always the optimist, he'd bait his hook carefully and throw out his line. Then he'd wait. Who knew? Maybe this fish would be the catch of the day... the week, the entire season. The possibilities were unlimited.

Whatever size or kind of fish he caught, he was always delighted. "Look at that!" he'd exclaim, assessing the new surprise. He'd shake his head slowly and chuckle softly, marveling that he had caught something after all. He never took his catches for granted, but appreciated each one with youthful enthusiasm.

Bringing his fish into the boat, he would hold it gently in his hands, being careful not to squeeze it too hard. Having no desire to eat the fish—catching it was the only thrill—he would slip the hook out of the fish's cheek quickly, wipe its mouth with a rag the way a parent pats a child, and then toss it back into the water. "If you want to do something right," he would say, "you have to do it slowly and carefully. Give each job the time and respect it deserves."

In business, Dad would say, there were difficult sales, and ones that practically fell in his lap. But those "simple" sales—the ones that seemed to be made only by opening an envelope or answering the telephone—really required hours of patience and dedication, and a very good memory. They were made by being available—often six or seven days a week—to answer questions, handle complaints, offer advice and stand behind a product.

There are different kinds of sales—like different kinds of fish. There are the small fry, the whoppers, and the ones that got away. But if you love selling, as my father did, you'll never want to stop trying to make one more "catch of the day"—one more sensational sale.

Furniture Today — May 18, 1985

Publisher's Note: "The author's father was a furniture manufacturer's representative for over 50 years in the New York City area. Last summer [1984], not long after a short fishing trip with his wife and daughter, he collapsed and died while on his way to call on a customer. His daughter penned the following tribute, which offers some insights to the people who make up an important part of the furniture industry."

ONE ITALIAN'S SECRET JEWISH HERITAGE

When my Sicilian father-in-law converted to Judaism at the age of sixty, he said he felt "a strong pull toward home, as if I always had a Jewish soul." Several years earlier, Joe had survived colon cancer and several complicated surgeries. His long recuperation gave him time to read, and to think. His second wife was Jewish, and Joe was curious about her religion. He began to pore over books about Jewish life, culture and history. He mastered Hebrew, studied Torah, gave up shrimp marinara and other dishes he'd adored, and insisted that his wife establish and keep a kosher home.

Eventually, Joe became chairman of the ritual committee of his synagogue. He was also the *gabbai*, assisting congregants at the *bimah*. He wrote a letter to his three children about his conversion. "I had no focus before, no compass spiritually," he explained; the Catholicism of his childhood had little impact on him.

Looking back, it's easy to see that Joe was exposed to elements of a Jewish past, although he didn't know it at the time. He was 11-years-old when he and his family left Castelmola, a small hill town above Taormina, but he never forgot a peculiar ceremony he watched on Friday nights: The priests would exit the old church carrying large and beautiful silver "relics" — which I would later learn were likely Torah embellishments — on pallets, and reverently parade them around the courtyard.

The procession moved solemnly, as the priests recited unintelligible, prayer-like words. "Nobody knew why they did this, but we knew it was important," Joe said. Furthermore, his mother's family history is murky and mysterious: His mother had been a foundling left on someone's doorstep in San Fratello, a Sicilian town that once had a Jewish population.

Five hundred years ago, about 40% of Sicilians and Calabrians were Jewish, according to Rabbi Barbara Aiello, the American-born founder of the Italian Jewish Cultural Center of Calabria. Tantalizing tidbits of what she calls "anecdotal evidence" persist today in subtle ways, often drawing the descendants of conversos — Jews who renounced their faith and adopted Christianity during the Spanish Inquisition — back to Judaism.

Jews probably came to southern Italy almost 2,000 years ago, especially around the time when the Maccabees, fearing annihilation by Antiochus's forces, sent scouts in boats into the Mediterranean to search for new homes. In recent years, the evidence of their arrival in Italy has been resurfacing. The remains of a fourth-century synagogue were found in Bova Marina, in Reggio di Calabria, and a mikveh of similar age was uncovered in Siracusa, Sicily. The island, 9,925 square miles, is situated alongside ancient trade routes and the straits of Messina, and would have been a good location for merchants and traders, most likely including Jews. At least three vestiges of the past endure in 21st-century Taormina: a pedestrian shopping walkway called *Traversa Degli Ebrei* (Street of the Jews);

a veterans hall with a three-sided second-floor balcony that suggests its probable history as a synagogue, and a municipal building with three plaster Stars of David prominently placed on its facade.

I thought about all this last summer, when I attended workshops on "The Archeology of Memory: Reclaiming Hidden Sephardic Jewish Roots," and "The Captives Return: *B'nai Anusim* (Children of the Forced Ones)" at the International Conference on Jewish Genealogy, held in Paris. As an amateur genealogist, I found the workshops intriguing. The speakers were Doreen Carvajal, an American journalist and author of <u>The Forgetting River: A Modern Tale of Survival, Identity, and the Inquisition</u>, and Jonina Duker, an educator and genealogist who is the main founder of the organization Kulanu, which reaches out to lost and dispersed Jewish communities everywhere.

Recalling my father-in-law's reflections, I understood what Carvajal meant when she talked about "ancestral memories." "The blood calls" is how Duker described Jewish souls finding their way back to the mainstream of the Jewish people.

The sessions also reminded me of the visit to Castelmola that my husband, sons and I made in 1990, and how startled we were to see leaded Stars of David in windows of the old church, which was about 800 years old. The leaded windows were set in stone panels on two sides of a bell tower.

Had this place once been a public building, or even a synagogue, in what had been the Jewish quarter? Later we would learn that when formerly Jewish structures were converted into churches or secular buildings during and after the Inquisition, superstitious inhabitants often preserved small signs of the past religion to guard against retribution (and soothe their guilt). Maybe it was bad luck to get rid of all the Judaica.

Carvajal — whose name in Spanish means "lost place," or "rejected" — sought answers to timeless questions: "Who am I?" and "Where do I really come from?" Driven to find answers, she moved with her family to an Andalusian town where her ancestors had lived long ago. There she would uncover hidden, ghostly intimations of Jewish life that had been whitewashed but not obliterated entirely, and by doing so she would confirm her Jewish heritage. Subsequently, she was able to track her DNA and was stunned, but not surprised, to learn that it was linked to Sephardic Jews in Spain.

Identity is often complicated and foggy. My family members also wondered about their ancestry. Could DNA testing help us? In 2009, at a conference on Italian-Jewish genealogy held in Manhattan, speakers confirmed the merits of DNA testing when "the paper trail no longer exists." Joe had questions, too; was he a Jew because he "felt" he was Jewish, or was it in his DNA? Was he descended from *neofiti*, as Italian *conversos* are called? As I watched my husband swab his father's cheek for a DNA sample, I couldn't help but think: Long ago, terrified Jews concealed their true identities to survive; now, our goal is to uncover them. A few weeks later, a DNA analysis confirmed that Joe's haplogroup belongs to a significant number of Jewish men and is especially common among Sephardic Jews. We still don't know for certain that Joe's heritage is Jewish, but the test brought us much closer to believing it to be so.

During a break at the conference, my husband and I met Rabbi Aiello, and my husband mentioned his father's recollections to her. "Did you say he came from Castelmola?" Aiello asked. "It was also my mother's birthplace. She, too, would describe to me the silver brought out on Friday nights. I believe they were the silver tops with tinkling bells that adorn the Torah, and also the breastplates — the decorations." Smiling, she added, "You know, probably, that whole town was Jewish!"

Joe smiled, too, when we repeated her story to him. Now 102 years old, he enjoys looking at old photos of Castelmola. Home never changes, even if you, yourself, have changed.

The Jewish Forward — February 1, 2013

HONOR THY FATHER?

I hated Father's Day when I was a kid. In the stormy family stew that was my almost-daily diet, "Father" meant "Sid," and that meant trouble.

My mother left Sid when I was two, and took my older brother, Jerry, and me with her to my grandmother's apartment in Queens, New York. Angry battles between my parents erupted with Vesuvian force as they fought about everything including court-ordered visitations that Jerry and I endured with Sid. We never knew when he might appear at Grandma's door, pounding furiously or climbing through her first floor windows if we didn't let him in "NOW!" He never forgave my mother's desertion, but he aimed his rage at safer targets—Jerry and me.

I was barely four when Sid put us on the outside fenders of his car and sped down Northern Boulevard. A few months later, he sent us (non-swimmers without life jackets) off in a rowboat that drifted in a bay while he stood on the shore. Another time, he smashed Jerry's eyeglasses and beat him up in a public park because he didn't answer a question. Gaping bystanders stared but didn't intercede because Sid insisted he was "just disciplining my boy." Even so, family court judges reduced but would not eliminate the visits. By the time I was eight, Jerry and I saw Sid only one hour a month, in the presence of a guard hired to watch us.

"Name the Ten Commandments!" Sid demanded. He often complained that we lacked religious educations. Quickly, I rattled off no killing, stealing, or wanting what your neighbor had. But I deliberately skipped "honoring" your parents, which I didn't understand at all. (Did that mean *him*?")

The visitations ceased when I was fifteen. Sid faded from my life but his specter lurked around the edges of my consciousness. Now and then, he sent me mildew-stained copies of old court records, and brief notes, but he never apologized for his actions. I wouldn't respond because Sid's punishment was never to know anything about me.

Eventually, after I joined a synagogue and began to study Jewish history, I learned about Amalek—the collective name of the tribe that attacked and harassed the Israelites during their forty years of wandering in the desert. And I realized that Sid was my Amalek—the evil malevolence you never spoke of but would not forget.

Decades passed until, through the flimsy grapevine that endures even in ruptured families, I heard that Sid was in a retirement home in California, and I decided it was time for me to show up. Maybe confronting Sid half-a-lifetime later would help me overcome my fears and sort things out. Only after I made flight reservations did I see I'd be there on Father's Day.

Seeing him was a shock. In my mind, Sid was still forty-something, with meaty hands and a smile that could turn into a sneer. Minutes passed before the scraggy old man comprehended who I was. "Susan?" he asked. "My Susan?" He lurched and embraced me, crying, drooling and laughing at the same time. I let him hug me but I couldn't hug back.

All afternoon, he tried to correct my "misconceptions about the past." He said, "You were so young, I was your father, you had no reason to fear me...."

No reason? I was exasperated. But my nightmarish recollections only produced cockeyed retorts: "Your memories are distorted." "Your mother brainwashed you." "I didn't kidnap your brother; he was confused."

He begged me to call him "Dad," but "Sid" was the best I could do. "Are you married?" he asked plaintively. "Do you work? Do you have children?" He had missed out on everything.

I had grappled with the Fifth Commandment long enough. Even if I could never forgive Sid's terrible, unhinged anger and violence in the past, I felt pity, now, for this pathetic 87-year old man. I couldn't honor him, but I could behave honorably. So I began to tell him about my life, and my family, especially his grandchildren.

I never saw Sid again, but until his death, sixteen months later, I wrote to him occasionally, and shared more stories. I didn't write to make Sid feel better, although I'm sure I did. Mainly, it was good and healthy for me.

The Jewish Week of New York — June 15, 2012

BEAUTIFUL, BORING DAYS

When a friend's four-year-old daughter fell out of a second-story window, she was hospitalized for several weeks with a concussion, two broken limbs, and numerous bruises.

"It was a month before we were sure she'd be all right," my friend recalled recently. "But during her slow recuperation, I kept remembering sitting with her a few days before the accident, helping her put some pieces in a puzzle. Suddenly, that was all I wanted—to be able to sit with my daughter and work on a puzzle with her. No grand plans—just a humdrum afternoon."

I began to think about "normal" times, those perfectly ordinary kinds of days when things are running pretty smoothly.

When my two sons were growing up, ordinary days were the mainstays of their existence. One-of-a-kind events did occur—happy occasions like winning a contest or starring in a school play, as well as the frightening, sad intrusions of some serious illnesses, the death of a pet, and a few broken bones. But most of the time, we were lucky; things were plain okay. This doesn't mean I took it all for granted, however. When Edward and Peter were little, part of me would always be on guard. Whenever we'd go out to the park or a store, I'd feel an unsettling twitch—where were they?—and then I'd look around and count them.

Fortunately, things usually are all right. Most days, our kids go off to school, we go off to work, and then we all come home again. The day is uneventful and satisfying, although we usually don't notice. It's only when something bad happens, as it did when my friend's child fell, that we remember all the good times we've had.

I started thinking about all this a few years ago, when my older son, Edward—sixteen-years-old, with a brand-new driver's license—took his friend for a ride on a winding country road. "Be back by dinnertime," I said as they pulled out of our driveway. I resisted the urge to add, "Be careful."

Edward telephoned an hour later, his voice tearful. "I totaled the car, Mom. I'm so sorry. I suppose I was driving too fast. We came around a curve, spun off the road, and almost hit a tree."

"But you're all right? Jon's all right?"

Edward sighed. "Yes, we're both fine. It's really amazing—we don't even have a scratch."

A few minutes after Edward called, my husband left to get him. (And Jon's dad went to get him.) I went into the kitchen to start dinner, although I knew I was not ready to do anything until I saw my son and knew he was all right. So I sat at the kitchen table, watching the sunlight filter through the trees outside our window, and my thoughts drifted back to when Edward was two-years-old. I had taught him the words to "You are My Sunshine," and told him it was true—he was like sunshine in my life.

After giving him a bath, I'd lift him out of the tub and wrap him in a towel. Then he'd put his damp arms around my neck and his legs around my waist, and we would dance.

"You are my sunshine," we'd sing, as we'd spin around the room. Times like these would never end, I felt.

Edward's car accident was just one of a series of crises we faced that year. Five weeks before, my stepfather had died suddenly, and left a gaping hole in the fabric of our family. And less than three months later, my husband became critically ill. I began to wonder if we would make it through these difficult days. And that's when I discovered the best way to confront them. Ordinary days—and our memories of them—often give us strength for the hard times we must face.

During the stressful time between my husband's medical diagnosis and his successful surgery, we lived as "ordinarily" as possible. Life continued with a predictable regularity, and that's what comforted us most.

Not long ago, I woke up on a particularly bleak morning. Rain was hitting the windows and rattling the gutters. "What a lousy day," I thought. The night before, Edward and Peter had gone out with their friends, driving on dark and slippery back roads. Somewhere between midnight and 1 a.m., in the state of semi-sleep I've learned is quite common among parents of teenagers, I had finally heard a car slowing down outside, then the back door opening and the familiar sounds of one son, then the other returning home at last.

Now they were asleep in their beds, and I looked at my husband, who was still in ours. He stretched luxuriously and pulled the blanket up around his shoulders. One hand reached out and patted the sheets I had just left, and he smiled as he felt their warmth beneath his touch. The rain continued to spatter against the house, but we were all inside and I had just "counted heads."

There'd be no grand plans today. Nothing special would happen, except the miracle of being together.

Working Mother — July 1992

OCTOBER TIMES

The two maple trees in front of my house have been shedding their leaves for the past few weeks. Sometimes, the leaves fall one by one, as singular and steady as drops of water. Other times, they descend in great messy clumps. After I rake them into nice tidy piles, new ones drop helter skelter on my lawn again, and brazenly remind me to get back to work.

While every new season causes me to look back as well as ahead, nothing makes me more nostalgic, more filled with a keen sense of longing for the past, than this period of late fall, and the coming onset of winter. It's not my favorite time of year; it lacks the hopes of spring, and the easy navigations of summer. But it's a season of renewal, as well as decay, and I've learned that fall is a gift as we head toward winter, offering us a soft passage into the dark months to come.

I'm sure the light has something to do with it. These days are brighter than the hottest days of summer, when the sun's hazy glow softens the edges of the world. Now the cool air is sharp as glass, and blazing fall colors awaken long forgotten memories. The earth strips down to its bare essentials, and bright hues fade into muted browns and greys. Recollections are stirred up and rustle like the leaves, as I lean on my rake and think of two small boys.

Years ago, my sons would race home from elementary school, clutching wide sheets of paper covered with glorious gobs of paint. The pictures flapped like flags as Edward and Peter ran, leaping over rocks and darting between trees.

For a long time, they brought home dozens of pictures, as numerous as the leaves, and as colorful, too. I'd beam with pride at my artists' great talents, and tape their creations to the refrigerator door. There were so many pictures, I never thought to save them; when the ones on display became soiled or ripped, they were easily replaced by newer masterpieces. But as the boys grew older, the "art work" changed to A+ papers and serious drawings illustrating book reports. Those incredibly beautiful, radiantly chaotic paintings had become tattered like old leaves and been discarded, and eventually, there were no more of them.

On fall weekends, our family raked leaves together. The boys helped briefly, but within minutes they were scooping up the leaves and tossing them wildly into the air. "Here we go!" shouted Edward, grabbing Peter's hand, and they hurled themselves fearlessly into the piles, until they were buried up to their heads. Sometimes, my husband and I jumped in, too, especially when most of the trees were bare and we knew this would be the last cleanup of the year. Who could resist that mad torrent of the leaves, as they swirled around us and crunched beneath our feet?

Raking leaves always meant that Halloween was coming, the night when children could howl like monsters and run fearlessly through our town's dark streets. Moonlight streamed through the trees' empty branches, creating eerie silhouettes and silvery long shadows. Costumes and routes were planned weeks in advance. Before the "big night," we would hollow out a pumpkin, carve slanted eyes and a toothsome grin, and gently place it on the front stoop of our house. My sons would pat the pumpkin when they went out trick-or-treating, and pat it again when they returned home.

By the time Edward and Peter were 12 and 10-years-old, I sensed pretty soon they'd feel too old for all of this. So I started a new tradition, and purchased two little pumpkins—one slightly smaller than the other—resembling the sizes my sons used to be.

When Edward and Peter were growing up, each season brought new beginnings and accomplishments. Achievements were as predictable as leaves falling down, and as each new milestone was reached and surpassed, all we ever did was anticipate more. But Halloween nights are as fleeting as childhood. I recall many times when we raked leaves, but I don't know when the very last times occurred. Like those splendid, abundant childhood paintings, they ended one day, and none of us noticed.

Eventually, my sons grew up, married, and moved away, and now the wealth of days we spend together has thinned down to intermittent times. This week, I placed a pair of orange pumpkins beside my front door. Each day, the sun sets earlier and earlier; in December, we will face the darkest time of year. But first will come Thanksgiving, that bright holiday of riches, when food must brim from everyone's plate, and families make long treks to gather together, before winter locks us into our separate seclusions.

Edward and Peter will be coming home for Thanksgiving with their wives and children, and in that time, we'll be together again. Perhaps one of them will notice the leaves on our lawn, pick up a rake, and tackle this small chore. It would be nice to see my sons raking leaves again. But I'd give anything to behold what I will never see again, the sight of them jumping into piles of leaves, and tossing them up into the air.

Victoria — September/October 2008

PARENTHOOD

Gordon family acting "goofy" 2009

IT'S YOUR PREGNANCY

"**W**e're pregnant!" my girl friend's husband, Pete, announced. He was grinning broadly, as they walked in the door.

Pete's expansive pride and good humor didn't stop him from eating his way through two bowls of guacamole with chips, downing three glasses of wine, and consuming an elaborate dinner topped off with a large portion of strawberry shortcake. My girl friend, on the other hand, turned the color of the dip when I offered her a taste, and took a nine-month raincheck on the drinks. For dessert, she picked at a few strawberries, apologizing for her queasiness.

"You both may feel pregnant," I remarked. "but it certainly doesn't 'show' on you, Pete."

When it comes to pregnancy, men are still running out to buy ice cream and pickles, and women are still throwing them up. And in hospital labor rooms around the world, women are going through the roof with each contraction, while the men just sit there, timing them. Enough of all this talk suggesting that men can be part of the "experience." Pregnancy is NOT an equal opportunity event!

Of course, your man will help you when you're pregnant. He'll dust a little, shop for the groceries, and even do some of the cooking. But pregnant he's not. So he can't share "the experience." I'm not talking about blissful dreams of tiny toes and little noses—those he can share.

I'm talking about uncontrollable flatulence, back strain and pinched nerves.

One man I know felt compelled to pack his own small suitcase, just like his wife, because he wanted to be "in touch" with every stage of her pregnancy. The night she went into labor, no one noticed that she grabbed the wrong bag. By the next afternoon, when their newborn son was sleeping peacefully nearby, the only things mommy could put on were a worn pair of jockey shorts and a splash of "Old Spice."

Natural childbirth classes can be interesting. You meet people you'll probably never see again, and discuss the most intimate details of your personal life. In between the panting and puffing, your nurse-instructor will rattle off fascinating facts about lollipops and odd uses for tennis balls. And in every class, there's always one early bird who delivered before graduation. The big moment comes when the new "papa" returns to tell the poor, pathetic still-pregnant members how thrilling it all was. That's what *he says*! She's shut up in a hospital room sunning her stitches with a heat lamp, and he's running around town buying stuffed animals and eating in restaurants with all their friends.

Let's face it—pregnancy should be center-stage time for a woman. A man can only be a supporting player. Although role-playing works well in modern families when it comes to cooking dinner and washing the dishes, childbearing remains a female occupation. A man who realizes this, who doesn't try so hard to identify with his partner's pregnancy, is most able to play the role for which he's really needed—that of a supportive, loving, and sensitive friend. He knows that a good friend remembers his partner barely slept last night because junior was practicing his left hook under her rib cage for five hours, so he gets up early to make her breakfast before leaving for work. He knows that a good friend helps the old girl out of her chair when she starts listing to one side, without spouting off long explanations of the biological reasons for her physiological changes. A woman in labor doesn't need her man studying the fetal monitors with a stopwatch. She needs him to rub her back and moisten her lips with a wet cloth.

Take it from me, fellas: dote on her like a maiden aunt—that's truly a shared pregnancy.

Mothers Today — September/October 1984

TRUST YOUR INSTINCTS!

...they're a very important part of parenting

During the time of my first pregnancy, my husband, Ken, and I read books, attended classes, and talked a great deal about what it would be like when we became parents. Our hands-on experience was limited, but we felt confident; taking care of a baby was a new skill we would master. After all, we reflected, we had learned to ride bicycles, speak French, and refinish furniture. All that took was hard work and dedication. This time, we would also have the strong motivation of love and, hopefully, some good-old common sense.

For the first six months of my pregnancy, we were extremely optimistic, but as the big event grew closer, we started to feel jittery. Maybe we didn't know so much, after all. Our parents had fulltime jobs, and none of our friends had babies. Who could we turn to, for help?

Three weeks before our baby was due, a generous check arrived from two sets of aunts and uncles. "Spend this money on something 'extra,'" they wrote us, "something you didn't think you could afford." We didn't have to think twice about that -

"A baby nurse!" we agreed. Now we could have live-in help for the first two weeks of our baby's life. Not only would a baby nurse give our newborn expert care and attention, she'd be our teacher, too. We telephoned a well-known, reliable agency in our area, and made arrangements.

The day our newborn son, Edward, and I came home from the hospital, a responsible looking woman in a crisp white uniform arrived with a small suitcase. Rest and sleep were what I needed, she told me, and she promised that I'd get plenty of it.

Edward was a spunky baby right from the start. He slept as little as possible, and ate as much as possible. Sometimes, he began to cry only one or two hours after his last bottle-feeding. His nurse, however, didn't pick him up all the time... and I, feeling very new and inexperienced, wasn't secure enough in my new role as mother to do it myself.

"He's been crying for ten minutes," I told the nurse one evening.

"You son has strong lungs. He was fed two and a quarter hours ago, and I just checked his diaper. He's fine."

"Then why is he crying?"

"He's learning to fall asleep," she replied, in a matter-of-fact tone.

"Learning to fall asleep"—that was a new one. Was falling asleep something a newborn had to learn? But what did I know? Here was the voice of authority telling me the facts in a calm and clear tone.

Edward was fine, except for his periods of crying. His nurse bathed, dressed, and rocked him, and when she fed him, she gave him as much as he wanted.

But when she left us, ten days later, Edward was still "learning" to fall sleep, and crying a lot in the process.

Timidly at first, and then with greater confidence, Ken and I started picking up Edward whenever he cried, and offering him his bottle, even if it was only a short while after his last feeding. Soon, he stopped crying so much, and he started sleeping more, too. And I started to think about everything that had happened.

I—who had been assertive as a college student and then assertive in my job, who had always demanded competence from every repairman and recompense from any faulty shopkeeper—had felt I knew nothing about baby care because I'd never been a mother before. And I let another person make all the decisions for me. Had I spent the past twenty-five years in a dark closet? Did I really have no sense of parenting and no sense of understanding what my baby wanted?

I should have realized that the nurse's responses were inappropriate, and I should have over-ruled her right away. Good instincts are natural, inborn qualities we all have. What I needed most in a baby nurse was someone who'd encourage me to follow my instincts and develop good judgment, not someone to dictate policies I was afraid to contradict.

Unlike most jobs in the outside world, parenting is often a solitary occupation. Because of this, new parents often make the mistake of accepting the advice of other people, even if our better instincts suggest they are wrong.

Now, our son, Edward, is growing up quite nicely, and so is his brother, Peter, who never was expected to "learn" to fall asleep. While I've forgotten the name of our first baby nurse, I'll always remember the expression she taught me. "Learning to fall asleep" has become one of my pet phrases. It's my label for hogwash and other nonsense which can negatively affect our lives. It's also my personal warning signal, reminding me to take charge of things and think for myself.

Expecting — Winter 1992-1993

THE WAR ON DIRT

I'm here to talk about plain old dirt, grime, goo, and slop, and how the birth of my first child changed me from a laid-back mopper-upper into a super neat and nutty mom. I became obsessed with dirt, and devoted my life to keeping it away from my squeaky clean, spotless new baby.

Soon after Edward was born, my mother-in-law offered him a plastic rattle. "Sweetheart," she cooed, "Look what Grandma's got for you!" Edward gurgled merrily and made a futile attempt to grab the toy.

"It's not washed yet!" I said, snatching it from my mother-in-law's hand. "But it's brand new," she answered. "Besides, he'll eat five pounds of dirt before he grows up."

Not my child, I vowed. Everything he touched would be perfectly clean. Even rattles wrapped in cellophane weren't clean until I washed them.

I sterilized his bottles, the nipples, and his little spoon. I scrubbed his baby tub before and after I bathed him. I washed his crib, and the nursery floor. Visitors had to remove their shoes before entering his room.

Basically, I believed there were two kinds of dirt: family dirt; and the dirt-of-the-rest-of-the-world. Controlling family dirt easy, as long as I was vigilant. But outdoors, the dirt-of-the-rest-of-the-world was everywhere. Mud splashed up brazenly from the sidewalk when Edward rode in his stroller, and scraps of paper swirled around him, touching that pristine face, that immaculate white blanket.

I cringed when big kids sidled over in the park and poked their sticky fingers into the stroller.

"Don't touch the baby!" I'd bark. Once, a little girl cried. She ran toward her mother, who dropped her newspaper and grabbed her daughter with ink-stained hands. "I'm sorry," I said. "She can look at the baby, but that's all. He's just so young and new." Most new mothers I met in the park felt the same way. "Did you see that?" asked my neighbor. "That little girl dropped her pacifier on the ground and her mother put it back in her mouth."

"Well, that kid in the sandbox, over there, was eating the sand and his nanny didn't do a thing!" remarked another mother.

But when our sons were seven months old, my neighbor called with startling news. "I'm not sterilizing anything anymore," she said. "Why not?" I gasped. "This morning, little Jimmy crawled out of the kitchen, while I was scrubbing his toys. I found him in the hall, sucking on the stroller wheels. Nothing's dirtier than that! I've had it!"

Not me. I resolved to be more diligent. Family dirt wasn't really dirty. If Edward licked a kitchen chair, or rubbed his hands on the bathroom door, he wasn't really touching dirt. The rest-of-the-world's-dirt was harder to keep away. I mean stranger's dirt, like a tarnished set of housekeys dangled before him by a lady in the supermarket. I was reaching for a bottle of laundry bleach when I heard him squeal, "Keeees!" and shove them in his mouth.

The older Edward grew, the more worn out I became. He threw things off his high chair constantly, and one time I almost gave his bottle back to him before I washed it. Another time, I found him underneath the couch, clenching a filthy piece of carpet fuzz. It was getting more and more difficult to keep up with him. By the time he was 2-years-old, I was pregnant with another baby.

My second son, Peter, was barely one month old when I found him nuzzling against a well worn child's sneaker, which Edward had tossed into the crib as a "gift." Soon, he was kissing his little brother's head and tiny fingers. I knew if I scolded him, it would turn him against this new addition to our family, so I took a deep breath and said, "This is only family dirt," but I knew it was more than that. Life had become more hectic. There was no way I could keep Peter's things spotless anymore.

By the time Peter was 16-months-old, he was following his older brother everywhere. One afternoon in the sand box in the park, Edward filled his plastic pail with sand, and Peter did the same. Edward patted the top edge neatly; Peter did the same. "Such wonderful children!" I thought. "What perfect little joys."

Edward lifted his pail above his head. So did Peter. Instantly, both boys laughed and dumped all the sand on to their heads.

"Exactly how much is five pounds of dirt?" I wondered.

American Baby — November 1990

A SMALL PLACE WITH PLENTY OF SPACE

I grew up in a small, one bedroom apartment. It hadn't been planned that way, but when I was two and my parents separated, my mother, brother and I moved into my grandmother's apartment, and stayed there for the rest of my childhood. Nights, Grandma slept on a studio couch in the living room; the rest of us slept in the bedroom, in three beds lined up in a row. My mother, looking for some humor in this sad situation, called our setup Ward A.

Although my mother and grandmother must have felt quite cramped, I never did. This small apartment was ... my home. I didn't question its size. Of course, I loved to visit friends who had their own rooms, so we could close a door and shut out everyone else. But home was home, and I had my own little hideaways.

The bedroom door couldn't swing open all the way because a large hook holding bathrobes and pajamas protruded from the back and hit the wall. But that little spot behind the door was a good place to sit and read, or just think. So was the space beneath the sewing machine table, or behind the wing chair that sat in a corner of the living room. From those places, I could quietly survey things, or simply focus on my own thoughts. When I slipped into one of my retreats, everyone left me alone. They didn't say, "Come out of there and sit on the sofa," or "Why are you reading in such a dark corner? Take your book over to a window." Even in a small apartment, I had plenty of room when I wanted it.

Not all children are as lucky as I was. A neighbor told me recently that she, too, had grown up in a cramped apartment. Her "bedroom" was the dining room alcove, separated from the kitchen and living room by an opaque curtain that was drawn with a cord. To me, she had lived like royalty—in a little nook entirely her own. But she hated it. "I never felt I was alone," she said. "I couldn't even cough without someone saying, 'Are you all right?' I desperately wanted my own private space. Even though I was given my own extension telephone when I was a teenager, I actually preferred talking on the phone in the kitchen because then I knew for sure when my family was listening."

All children need space, but it's the space inside that they really need—room to dream, think or just be by themselves. Outside space is never as important. Sometimes, in fact, close living has advantages. I always fell asleep to sounds of the living room radio or TV, Mom and Grandma talking to each other, or on the phone. Those sounds were very comforting to me. I don't think I would have wanted to sleep in a quiet room, far away from everyone else. If I woke up in the middle of the night, frightened by a nightmare or by strange noises outdoors, the steady, rhythmic sounds of my mother and brother sleeping nearby always helped to calm me down.

Today, I live with my husband and two sons in a roomy house in the suburbs. Each boy has his own bedroom, and neither one remembers his first years of childhood, when we lived in a city apartment and space was tight. But our older son recalls when we first moved to our "up-and-down house" when he was 5-years-old. At first, he couldn't fall sleep in his upstairs room unless my husband or I were upstairs, too. Our son told us that he felt terribly alone "up there," and worried about noises in the night.

No amount of parental comforting short of sitting in his room or in the hall nearby could make him relax. So I'd sit with him, explaining that Dad and I were not far away, although it seemed that way. I also said it was the grownups' responsibility—not the children's—to listen for noises and protect the house. He could go to sleep because we would be "on guard" for him. For a long time, however, nothing worked except sitting upstairs with him, or in my bedroom down the hall.

That first year in our house, when we all were adjusting to living in a large space, we rented a small beach cottage for our summer vacation. After the boys went to bed at night, my husband and I would read or talk quietly in the living room, only a few feet away from them in the bedroom they shared. Our younger son fell asleep easily, as he usually did at home, but now so did our older son. He could hear our voices and listen to us turning pages, and he liked knowing that we were right there. Who could blame him? I had been the same, when I was a child. I just needed him to remind me.

Working Mother — September 1986

JOYS OF SENDING CHILDREN OFF TO CAMP

After spending countless summers sitting around 12-inch-deep wading pools, visiting nearby beaches chosen for their proximity to bathroom and snack-bar facilities and making endless trips to nature centers, local zoos and day camps, many parents start seriously thinking about sleep-away camp for their children. No need to take a vacation this summer—the kids will be going out of town instead!

Where will they be going? That's a complicated question, and it will take hours, weeks, possibly months of debate and discussion before the (hopefully) perfect camp is found. If you are a parent with children of summer-camp age, read on!

Let's face it. You and your spouse haven't been alone for an extended period of time since Mom went into labor nine years ago this spring. It's not unreasonable for you to want to recapture the magic of those early, peaceful years, long before soccer practices, piano recitals, orthodontist appointments and Girl Scout cookie drives took over your lives.

Summer camp was invented for parents as well as children. And while many children do have a happy and active summer, on the whole it is parents who enjoy summer camp the most!

No parent, however, is permitted to send his or her child away for the summer without feelings of remorse and wrongdoing. Guilt appears when you first send for camp catalogues, and it increases in its intensity as you:

- Fork over the first few hundred dollars as a "nonrefundable" deposit;

- Shut the lid on the overstuffed camp trunk, which contains enough newly purchased clothing to outfit an entire village of dependent children living in the Andes;

- Mail off your first letter three days before your child leaves for camp, "just so he'll have something from home to greet him on the day he arrives;"

- Wave goodbye as the camp bus pulls out of the parking lot;

- Go home to strip the sheets from your child's recently vacated bed, knowing it can now "air" for eight weeks straight;

- Book two weeks at an "adults only" resort.

Guilt does not appear suddenly; it creeps up on you stealthily all winter long and can hang over your head for the entire summer vacation. Don't be alarmed. It disappears with miraculous speed the moment the kids step off the bus in late August.

Never choose a camp that your child begs to attend. Camp is supposed to be something children hate, something for them to cry and complain about in every letter home ("The food stinks, the counselors hate me and I almost drowned again in the lake today.") Furthermore, parents who decide to send their kids to "all-boy" or "all-girl" camps in the hopes of keeping their kids' minds off members of the opposite sex are wasting their time. Boys at a camp in Maine were discovered to have paddled, portaged and hiked six miles in one night just for 20 minutes on the back porch with girls at a ''nearby'' camp. Girls at a camp in Vermont were caught sneaking off camp grounds at 3 a.m. during a hailstorm because they had ''promised'' waiters at a local resort they'd drop in ''whenever we have a little free time.''

Although most camps offer a wide range of athletic, dramatic, and arts and crafts activities, some parents feel the need to consider specialty camps for their progeny. Are specialty camps a worthwhile alternative? Before you sign on the dotted line, ask yourself:

- Is it really necessary for anybody to play six hours of soccer every day for three weeks?

- How ''wild'' is life at a wilderness camp? Is it reasonable to expect kids to forage for their own food, when all that's available are roots and berries?

- Can a child at a ''Strictly Sailing'' camp survive five days of unrelenting rain and wind?

- Is riding the rapids a maturing experience for someone whose fear of water has been nothing less than all-consuming?

- Can anyone—except a horse—really enjoy the daily routine of slogging through fresh manure?

Meeting the camp's director can be an eye-opening experience. Be suspicious of directors who interview prospective families in downtown hotels that smell of cabbage cooking on hot plates. The interior of a camp director's meeting rooms corresponds (with frightful accuracy) with the decor of his summer cabins. View critically a director who playfully cuffs your kid on the chin and says, "Call me 'Uncle.' " And never trust a director who tells you no child has ever gone home from his camp unhappy, or no counselor has ever been fired for improper behavior.

Directors who require campers to wear camp uniforms all the time say that their dress code "equalizes" the campers. Not so. It rarely takes kids more than two hours to establish a pecking order in their bunks. Clothes may be the same, but items such as portable radios and tape cassettes, fiberglass fishing poles and graphite tennis rackets are clear indications of social and monetary rank.

Avoid camps that do not participate in inter-camp games. The director may tell you he is too concerned about his campers' safety and doesn't like to let them off the campgrounds, but his true feelings have nothing to do with safety—he's afraid to let his kids see another camp, where they might talk to other campers. ("You have showers in your bunks? You have running water? Electricity? Roofs?")

Many camps today offer four- and eight-week sessions. Which length of time is best? Some parents choose to send their kids to camp for four weeks because they feel guilty about sending them away. Others think they need time to take the family on a vacation after the kids come home. And others are concerned about the financial costs.

All these justifications will seem pitifully inadequate in retrospect. Mark my words: the kids will be back soon enough. September will return, and it will be reliably followed by October, November, December (you know the rest), when they will be home home home (home with their complaints, home with their colds, home with all their "drive me/take me/buy me/watch me" requests).

So break the bank, stretch your budget as far as it can go and send the kids for a full eight weeks. So what if it means eating day-old bread and food out of dented cans—you'll be eating in peace and quiet.

Note to campers: kids who plan to spend eight weeks at a camp that offers four- and eight-week sessions have a strong advantage over the second group of campers who arrive in late July—pale, naive, and totally uninformed. (Even a "new kid" becomes an "old timer" if he or she has been at camp since the beginning of the summer.)

Parents, as well as campers, should prepare for the campers' day of departure. It's not uncommon for parents to stand around in shock as the buses pull out of the parking lot. A couple from New York, alone at last after eleven years of servitude, had to be warned to get out of the sun after three quarters of an hour.

One mother, unable to shake the habit of "tidying up" after her children, trotted behind their bus, sweeping the concrete roadway. And one husband almost caused his fragile wife to have a coronary when he volunteered to shop for new bathroom curtains. ("I don't know why I suggested it," he later recounted, "but all of a sudden there just didn't seem to be anything to do on a Saturday afternoon without the kids. I got so used to running to baseball games, dance programs and swim meets, that for a while I had no idea what I wanted to do!")

We send our children to camp so we can miss them, and—after a well-deserved vacation from daily loads of laundry, astronomically high grocery bills and the deafening roar of rock radio stations—finally welcome them back into our loving arms.

Will this be any way to spend a summer? You bet it will!

The New York Times —June 20, 1982

PUTTING TOGETHER THE CAMP TRUNK

For parents of sleepaway camp-bound youngsters, springtime has a special significance—it's the season to shop for and pack the camp trunk.

Trunks are acquired in different ways. If you're lucky, you may inherit a slightly battered but still serviceable hand-me-down model from a friendly neighbor or relative. Otherwise, reasonably priced trunks can be purchased in discount department stores, small luggage shops or—that staple of camping supplies—the local Army-Navy store. If you're interested in status, Louis Vuitton offers a snappy beige and brown version, complete with "LV" logo, for only $4,500.

How do you pack the camp trunk? With great thought, a little psychology and a lot of determination. An informal survey among veteran trunk packers in Westchester NY has produced the following guidelines for beginners:

1. Disregard quantities of clothing listed in the camp-clothing folder. This means you should first assess your child's personal dress code. Has he worn only two pairs of pants, three shirts and one ragged pair of sneakers all winter? Then he doesn't need the recommended seven pairs of pants, twelve shirts and three pairs of shoes. If you have a daughter who practically lives in leotards, also

disregard camp suggestions that you pack just one; give her five leotards and totally omit the pajamas.

If you decide to follow the camp-clothing folder, be warned—one mother found store tags still attached to two-thirds of her child's summer wardrobe.

2. Toilet kits are overrated. Toothpaste, toothbrushes, soaps, mouthwashes, deodorants, shampoos and other ''vital'' bathroom articles may be purchased and packed along with sworn oaths by your child that they will be used regularly, but an amazing number of supplies will come home untouched. How the average camper can use less than half a cake of soap and only one teaspoon of shampoo in two months is an interesting question many parents will wrestle with late in August.

3. A variety of hats is essential. When worn regularly, they virtually eliminate the need to pack a comb and brush.

4. Do not pack food items. Here is one issue about which most parents and camp directors agree. Unfortunately, campers have different attitudes about good nutrition and, with the skill of a gun moll smuggling saws into San Quentin, they will stash chewing gum, corn-chip bags and candy into the tiniest crevices of their trunks.

5. Name tape everything. Some people think this means toothbrush bristles and the soles of their children's feet, but my list is more realistic: it includes orthodontic retainers; pierced earrings; flashlight batteries and postage stamps.

6. Paste a complete list of clothing and supplies inside the trunk lid. This will enable you and your child to count up all the items lost during the summer. Don't be surprised if he or she returns home minus 3 ½ pairs of socks, all the washcloths and that hooded poncho you forced him to buy, knowing quite well that he hated it.

Also, your list will help you identify unfamiliar garments—the once-white tennis shorts that were messily dyed orange during Color War, the lace-trimmed bathrobe apparently chewed up and spat out by the camp laundry, and the good gray slacks irreparably altered to become the Scarecrow's trousers for the camp production of "The Wizard of Oz."

7. Leave space for the trip home. You may pack everything neatly and with great efficiency (heavy items on the bottom, all soft and breakable things on top), but in all likelihood, your child will do his return packing himself. Counselors don't pack for anyone old enough to do it by himself (clearly a subjective decision, but a quick poll reveals the median age to be 7) and play an active role only on the final day, when the counselor finds the fattest kid in the group and has him sit on the trunks, so they can be closed and locked.

One boy, who spent the winter months at school tossing paper balls into the class wastebasket fifteen feet away, packed his trunk with the same carefully developed style. One girl, who had completed eighteen crafts projects, including six oversize papier-mâché African masks, used her untouched linens to wrap her creations. Nobody warned her that poster paint, left in a warm, slightly damp location, soon begins to "bleed" and can speedily tie-dye an entire set of sheets and towels.

In the end, all items your child is unable to stuff into his trunk will appear on his person when he steps off the camp bus. The temperature may be 90 degrees but the layered look will definitely be "in": looking like a bunch of shifty shoplifters slipping out of a discount-clothing store, your child and his buddies will be wearing at least two jackets, three shirts and a bathing suit under their jeans.

Consider yourself lucky if no beetles or other crawling things creep out of sleeves, cuffs or collars before you can throw everything into the washing machine.

The New York Times — May 31, 1981

A CHILD'S GUIDE TO SURVIVING THE FIRST SUMMER OF CAMP

Every summer, a new crop of youngsters departs for sleep-away camp for the first time. Being away from home is a difficult adjustment in itself, but when coupled with the stresses of being a "new kid" in camp, the situation can become unbearable.

To gain some insight into this predicament, an informal survey was conducted among "old" campers who live in our county and will soon be leaving to spend another season hiking, swimming, playing on sports teams, singing around campfires, performing in dramatics and making life miserable for the "new kids" in their groups. Reluctantly, and only with firm assurances that no names of camps or campers would be given, they disclosed some eye-opening information. The following is a presentation of the old campers' attitudes: may the "new kids" beware!

Success at summer camp depends on how fast a camper can get off the camp bus, dash to the group cabin and select the best bed to sleep in for the summer. "Best beds" are never placed under a hole in the roof, and their frames are supported by four legs. They are as far as possible from the counselor's bed, and as close as possible to the bunk cache of snack food. Also, except in special situations, when out-of-the-way nooks are used to store contraband or plot midnight raids, "best beds" are not found in corners, which are popular spots for spider nests and bat droppings.

For these reasons, old campers know that it is a good idea for them to sit with a group of "new kids" on the bus ride to camp. The new arrivals will listen to every word you say, and follow any advice you care to offer. Arriving at camp, you can easily steer them down the path toward the lake (just tell them it's a secret shortcut to the bunks), giving yourself plenty of time to go pick out your sleeping location.

Another good reason to sit with the new camper (or campers) is to establish trust. New campers—like newborn infants—attach themselves permanently to the first pair of eyes that focus sympathetically on them. Several hours of bus "friendship" will guarantee you a whole summer of:

- First dibs on all the new camper's packages from home;

- Rights of first choice on all the new camper's "Peanuts," "Doonesbury" and "Garfield" books;

- A loyal "lookout" or "fall guy" in many crucial situations. If you were unable to sit next to a new camper en route to camp, it will not be difficult to spot him or her once you get there. "New kids" are the only campers who arrive with a complete camp uniform. This means their trunks contain an exact count of everything on the camp list, and nothing more. In addition, their camp uniforms are always too large for them because, at this point, they actually anticipate coming back next year!

If the words "indoctrinating the new kid" have a nasty ring to them, we are only being realistic. Who else would believe:

- Every camper must swim twenty laps across the lake fully dressed before he or she can take out a rowboat;

- The bunk person responsible for cleaning up after the late night food fights has traditionally been the camper who sleeps next to the bathroom door (or to the right of the front door, or under the big window or wherever the new camper's bed happens to be);

- Baby doll pajamas may be used for sleeping only after they have been worn once around the mess hall in the moonlight. (It is vital for old timers to state unequivocally that their baby dolls already saw the stars, last year.)

Note: Keeping the new arrivals from using such facilities as the rowboats—until they swim twenty laps—frees this equipment for the use of "old campers" and cuts down on the pinch of supplies. ("You want a basketball? Sorry, you can't use one until you hop around the court forty times. It's a tradition!")

Tradition and stories about previous camp seasons play a big part in the manipulation of the new campers. Old hands are forever telling new campers, "It was better last year." They may be referring to things as varied as the food, the weather or the counselors, but the message is always the same: you will never know how good camp was before you arrived, and it will never be that way again.

So how can a "new kid" survive the first summer at camp? Here are some tips from former new campers who made it through their first seasons:

- Infiltrate the crowd of old timers on the bus ride to camp, and strictly avoid sitting—or socializing—with the other new campers;

- Soil, stain, bleach and crush your new camp uniform, and wear it only when absolutely necessary;

- Never confess that you're totally new to camping. Casually drop vague hints about "atrocities" you and other buddies committed at another camp last summer. This information will help you shed the stigma of "new camper" by making you an old camper—who was pretty tough and independent—somewhere else;

With luck, your efforts will pay off—and you will return next year to bedevil subsequent new campers.

The New York Times — July 10, 1983

PARENTS' GUIDE TO VISITING DAY AT CAMP

There is a short but special season of the year that fits neatly between the beginning of July and the end of August. It is the time when parents of children away at summer camp have finally adjusted to tiny loads of laundry, sinfully small grocery bills and plenty of peace and quiet, and it precedes the period when they start dashing off to concert halls, R-rated movies, getaway weekends for two and other "adult" activities—before the kids come home.

By the middle of summer, the family dog has reluctantly left his post at the kitchen door, having given up hope of seeing his favorite people trooping in at 3 o'clock. Even the family car has accepted the new routine; it has stopped turning automatically onto its old routes—the roads to school, the orthodontist, barbershop, soccer field, dancing lessons and birthday parties. It now knows the way to art museums, antiques shows and Japanese restaurants that specialize in sushi. And it appreciates taking a nice, relaxing drive without having its back seat battered by juvenile wrestling and rioting.

At this special time, when the eight weeks of summer camp so beautifully balance—four weeks gone and four more weeks to go—parents jump into cars, planes, trains and buses and run off to the country, eager to be the first adults their children will see at camp on Visiting Day.

The kids are encouraged by the camping staff to play catch, clean their bunks or "just play quietly" while waiting for Visiting Day to begin, but soon after breakfast, they all start drifting toward the main gate. A glimpse of one's parents—or the parents of a friend—can give instant status to someone with sharp eyes.

Many things should be considered by parents as they make their way from the parking lot, lugging lawn chairs, blankets and shopping bags filled with goodies. The following information is presented as a guide to these parents:

1. Be prepared for some changes in your child's appearance. Do not cry, "Good grief! They're starving you! You must have lost at least 10 pounds!" Even if your daughter (on whom you have spent close to $2,000 for this summer in the sun) looks like an inner-city advertisement for "send this poor child to camp," don't admit it in front of her. Also, don't comment on other peculiarities; try to ignore tattoo marks (they'll probably wash right off with nail polish remover), experimental hair-dos and recently pierced ears.

2. Remember, you are at camp for only one day. Control the urge to speak your mind. Lay off the scolding. Do not say, "You needn't call home collect every time you get a stomach ache. This camp has two competent nurses," even if you're bursting to do so. Within a week, you'll be swearing they have acute appendicitis and are afraid to let you—or anybody else -know.

Do say, "Things are very quiet at home. Most of the time we just sit around the house and say how glad we are that you're out of the hot city."

3. When you visit your child's cabin, studiously avoid any close examination of his or her toilet kit. The toothpaste, soap and shampoo you assiduously purchased in June may still be unwrapped. Furthermore, delving into a dirt-encrusted clothes cubby might excite a field mouse or other country creature that may have made a home for itself in some warm, wet socks.

4. If you must take food, don't take anything perishable. Aunt Helen's chopped liver may be a family treat at home, but it will quickly turn to moldy paste in summer heat. If you buy candy or other snack items, don't buy more than the amount your child will be able to stuff into his or her mouth that night. It is an unwritten custom among campers to gorge themselves on as many food treats as possible within 24 hours after Visiting Day.

5. Do not attempt to give your son a midsummer haircut. He probably thinks he was already scalped in June and his hair is just beginning to "grow in." Also, do not tell him his kid sister stuck her hands into his fish tank "just to pet them, Mommy," and three swordtails died from shock. The bad news can wait until he comes home from camp.

6. You may have received one or two frantic letters written the week before Visiting Day, with outrageous requests such as "Please bring the dog. We can smuggle her into my bunk during General Swim," and "You've got to get me out of here! This is the third night I've had to sleep under the bunk!" Don't let these pleas get to you on Visiting Day. It's normal to expect some dissatisfactions.

One mother spent an entire visit listening to a litany of complaints from her 10-year-old daughter. The food was horrid. The other kids hated her. The camp director was always yelling and the head waterfront counselor had threatened to drown her if she didn't master the Australian crawl. By the end of the day, the mother was reduced to jelly. Wondering if she should tell the child to hurry and pack her bags, she tremblingly hugged her and kissed her on the cheek. Before she could speak, her daughter was off, running down the camp trail back to her bunk. Over her shoulder, she called, "when I come back next year, I want to be in Bunk 8!"

7. Do not bring any treasured possessions from home. You will immediately hear, "Let me see it, let me see it," from your child's bunkmates, and the next words may regretfully be, "Oh, I'm sorry, I didn't mean to break it..."

8. Be sure to wear comfortable, closed-toe shoes. One mother wearing high-heeled pumps speared as much grass and litter with her stiletto spikes as an overzealous sanitation worker in Central Park. One father, all decked out in new, imported sandals, spent half the car ride home picking gravel and tar off the soles of his feet.

9. Do not leave the camp grounds, especially if you're not familiar with the territory. At one camp in Massachusetts, picnic lunches were offered to campers and their families. A 12-year-old boy invited his folks to eat with him at a "special place" he had discovered in the woods. "Look at the grass," he told them, "it's so warm and moss-like." They spread his jelly-roll blanket down on the ground and rubbed their hands on the soft, furry surface. Lunch was eaten and while everyone was relaxing, the head counselor appeared. "Hi," he said, and then he paused nervously. They could tell bad news was coming. "I

hate to tell you this," he fidgeted, "but you're sitting on top of the camp cesspool."

10. At departure time, don't be surprised if, having seen what all the other parents brought their children, your child has made a new list of "must-haves" for you to send by mail.

11. Make your goodbyes short. Nobody likes to pry his own kid's fingers off the car fender, or shut the car door on a forlorn face. One family drove three miles before they discovered what the "extra weight" was in the trunk. Your best bet is to leave a half-hour before Visiting Day concludes, so you and your kids aren't stimulated by the tearful separations around you. Besides, by leaving early you'll beat the other parents back to the city and have more time to enjoy your remaining weeks alone!

The New York Times — July 26, 1981

MY CAR POOL BLUES

Priscilla got a jump on the fall carpooling season last year when she called me the previous June. "Just getting things in order for next term," she began. "I want make sure you have places for my children in the new schedule."

I knew why she was eager. She lives on a cul-de-sac on the edge of town. Nobody passes her house.

"Look, Priscilla," I told her. "school's almost over. Who wants to think about music lessons, soccer games and swim meets now? Let's talk around Labor Day, okay? I promise there'll be spaces for your kids."

Now I was stuck. But I decided not to tell the other drivers until September, when I called everyone on the list.

"I can only drive on Monday this year," said Midge. "And I have to take Mandy to her dancing lessons; would you mind taking my Mitchell to his swim meets? I'll switch with you next May... you better write this down...."

"Midge!" I screamed. "Wait a minute! We're just starting the season. If you want Monday, you've got it."

"That's great!" she said. "Will it be the same group as before?"

"I'm not sure," I fibbed.

"Has anything changed?" she pressed.

"Yes," I admitted. Why did I have to deal with this, anyway? "The Edwardsons moved away. Remember?"

"Oh, yes. Well, who can we get? It must be someone convenient. I hate going out of my way for just one kid."

"It'll be two kids."

"What two kids?"

"Priscilla's."

""Good grief! I'm not driving all the way over to Cranberry Drive."

"It's only once a week. She called me last June, and I had to say yes."

"Okay," Midge relented, "but she better be on time."

Next, I called Flossie who chose Wednesdays. Flossie was a honker. It didn't matter if she was early or late or if your kids were already waiting outside. Flossie always honked her car horn.

Daisy was last on my list. The year before, she had chosen Mondays which seemed fair until Midge noticed that many school holidays occurred on Mondays and grabbed that day. Never one to be quiet when a point was to be made, Daisy accosted Midge in the supermarket and suggested we occasionally take our turns, to "even things out."

Thankfully, Daisy gave me no trouble. "Since Midge has Mondays this year," she sniffed, "Fridays will be all right for me."

And Priscilla, much cheerier now that she was sure she had a spot, said, "You've no idea what a hassle it is living on the outskirts of town."

"I'll soon find out," I said, sighing.

"Oh, yes," she said with a giggle. "I guess you will!"

In retrospect, it went more smoothly than I had expected. We all took our turns driving to Priscilla's house, but those trips only took extra time, not aggravation. Midge not only benefited from all those Monday holidays, but she got one "Snow day" too. Flossie honked and honked until a cold rainy day in March, when the horn stuck and kept on blaring. A cruising policeman gave her a ticket for disturbing the peace.

I drove on Thursdays and, although I got a day-off on Thanksgiving, it never snowed on my day. Priscilla drove regularly and reliably on Tuesdays. She was never late and was the only car pooler who didn't call at the last minute to switch with another driver. This June, in fact, I'm calling Priscilla myself. I'm not taking any chances of losing her.

McCall's — October 1986

BLUEBELL & EDWARD

Our parakeet, Bluebell, died years ago, but my son Edward still keeps his little bird's mirror and bell in the top drawer of his desk. He and Bluebell formed a special bond that Edward will never forget.

Bluebell was a spunky bird. He had bright blue-and-white feathers that he kept perfectly preened, and a circle of black dots around his neck. We bought him when Edward was six-years old, and my younger son, Peter, was four. The boys were starting a new school year, and it seemed like the right time to bring a pet into our home. Dogs and cats were ruled out because of allergies, so we opted for a parakeet because we heard they were great "people pets."

Within weeks, we had taught Bluebell to sit on our fingers, shoulders, and heads. We also decorated his cage with a little mirror that had a red bell attached to the bottom. Soon, the "other bird" in the mirror became the passion of Bluebell's life.

At first, we thought we should keep Bluebell in one of the children's bedrooms, but each boy wanted it to be in his. Instead, everyone agreed to put Bluebell in the small playroom near the kitchen, so that we all could enjoy him.

I spent a lot of time in the kitchen preparing meals or working at a desk in the corner. When the boys started school, I found myself alone at home for the first time in six years. It might have been too quiet... but I had Bluebell. He'd chirp incessantly at his mirror image—sometimes in soft, melodious tones, other times quite vociferously. He would bang the mirror with his beak and poke the bell with his foot. Every time he shook the mirror, the "other bird's" animated response made Bluebell dance around his cage gleefully.

After school, Edward and Peter ate snacks, played games, and did their homework in the playroom. Bluebell loved sitting on their shoulders so he could warble sweet nothings into their ears, or gently tug on their shirt collars and sleeves. Then he'd hop onto the play table and strut around over their books. Both boys were convinced that he helped them with their homework by pecking at the correct answers to multiple-choice questions!

Like many siblings, Edward and Peter squabbled sometimes, and verbal disagreements could erupt into shoving and pummeling matches. Fists flew, but most blows were harmless (causing pain and anxiety only to their mother). They knew how to be careful when Bluebell was around; rough-housing was okay, but hurt their bird? Never!

Few children were afraid of this merry bird, although some grownups felt differently. One Thanksgiving, my three-year-old nephew, Robby, climbed down from his dining room chair, wandered into the playroom, and opened Bluebell's cage door. Having overheard the noise and activity, Bluebell was eager to join the party. He flew out of the playroom and headed straight for the dining room. How such a small bird could resemble a dive-bomber is unbelievable to me, but two grandmothers and one aunt gaped in horror when they spotted him coming. Seeing them shriek and duck their heads was like watching a scene from Alfred Hitchcock's movie, *The Birds*.

That winter, Edward became very sick with pneumonia. Day after day he lay in bed, his head resting on three pillows to help him breathe more easily. He slept poorly, waking at night because his chest hurt. I often sat with him—reading his favorite stories to him, or playing quiet games with him. The weather was dreary, rain pounded on the windows, and the skies outside were dark and gloomy.

Sharing Edward's room was "Dr. Soothee," a pathetically homely little rag doll he had created from old stockings stuffed with soft cloth, with fabric scraps for its eyes, ears, and weak smile. Edward thought Dr. Soothee would help make him well. But my husband had another idea.

"Look who's here," he said one evening as he carried Bluebell's cage into Edward's room. Edward's face brightened for the first time in days. When we opened Bluebell's door, he jumped to the edge of his cage and looked at Edward. Then he looked back at the "other bird" in the mirror. In one instant a decision was made. Bluebell fluttered his wings and flew toward Edward. Alighting on the bed, Bluebell cocked his head to one side and stared at Dr. Soothee, who was on Edward's lap. What—and who— was this?

Bluebell squawked, but of course, the doll was silent. Bluebell squawked again, but the doll didn't move. With what can only be described as a worried look on his tiny face, Bluebell marched straight up Edward's quilt, leaped into the air, and landed on Dr. Soothee. He inspected the doll with the same gentle care he used with children, which meant pecking but not jabbing, stroking but not scratching. Finally, he concluded that the doll was okay.

"I know I'll sleep tonight, if Bluebell is watching," said Edward. So we placed the birdcage beside his bed and left the cage door open, giving Bluebell the option of staying in or venturing out.

Bluebell stayed by Edward's side all night. The next morning, I tiptoed by Edward's room and peeked in. Dr. Soothee had fallen to the floor; maybe Edward had knocked the doll off his bed accidentally, or maybe ... it had been pushed over the edge by someone else.

Bluebell wasn't talking. In fact, he was still asleep. No bigger than a small ball of fluff, he was encamped at the foot of Edward's bed with his head tucked under one wing.

When Edward woke up, I took his temperature. For the first time in days, it was normal.

Over the years, Nurse Bluebell visited other sickrooms in our house, and never left his post until the patient felt better. Finally, when he was almost eight-years-old, Bluebell became sick and no vet could save him. Now, it was Edward's and Peter's times to be nurses, and they took turns watching him. They cupped the little bird's body carefully in their hands, and held him close to keep him warm.

On the day that Bluebell died, I remembered why we bought him long ago. We thought caring for a bird would be relatively easy, and that it might be fun to have a pet in our house. What we didn't anticipate was how deeply we would grow to love him, and how much he would become a part of our lives.

Parents — November 1985

MY HALLOWEEN CONFESSION

My sons are not going trick-or-treating this year. The ghostly goblin and the tramp are choosing to stay at home. They're probably right. At thirteen and fifteen, they've gotten too big to go out on Halloween night. Even last year, the boys began to feel foolish. The night belongs to the little kids, they told me—little kids who still believe the whole thing is real.

My boys may think they're "over the hill," but I still love this October holiday with its heady atmosphere of spookiness and suspense. And I love seeing ordinary neighborhood children transform themselves into super-heroes, scruffy hoboes, fiendish witches, and fairy-tale princesses.

For a long time, my sons loved the holiday too. When they were younger, they began thinking about Halloween as soon as school started in September. Within weeks, they'd begin making their costumes, planning their route, and praying that the weather would be good—cool, crisp, dry—but knowing that nothing short of a hurricane would keep them home that special night.

For a few years, they wore different outfits, but then they settled into their goblin and tramp getups. The goblin wore a white bedsheet covered with paintings of ghosts, witches, haunted houses, and smashed pumpkins. The tramp put on shabby pants, an unmatched pair of shoes, his grandfather's old felt hat, and a buttonless jacket. They didn't wear masks. Instead, they applied gobs of sticky makeup in madcap fashion, until all you could see were the tramp's brown eyes, surrounded by soot-smeared skin, and the goblin's bright blue eyes, which were the only bits of color on his chalk-white face.

On Halloween Day, anticipation was at its highest. Each year they predicted they would ring more doorbells, run farther, stay out later, and terrify more neighbors than ever before. All the children in our neighborhood went out in dark scary costumes on Halloween night, collecting treats, or money for a charity. Ringing doorbells, they were rewarded just by chanting those magic words: "Trick or Treat!" The older ones tried to appear serious (but often giggled), and the younger ones squealed and clutched each other's hands. Under lopsided hats, their wide eyes revealed their amazement to be part of this magical night.

One year, I got so caught up in all this enthusiasm, I impulsively bought a pair of hideous monster gloves, complete with warts, oozing sores, scabs and gnarled nails.

"You bought them for yourself?" my older son asked. "Halloween is a children's holiday" Then he paused. "Isn't it?"

"I don't see why it's only for children," I remarked. "After all, while you trick-or-treat, I stay home and answer the door. And won't those kids be surprised when this hand doles out the treats!"

My son agreed, and together we plotted ways to make the scene even scarier. He suggested I keep the foyer dark, with one flickering candle the only light. Then, when the doorbell rang, I would call out in my best "witchy" voice, "Who's there?" with a cackling laugh. It was terrific.

That's why this year, when my two sons have decided they're too old for Halloween, I'm not ready to give it up. I plan to turn on the porch light, turn off the hall light, wrap up little bundles of cookies and candles, stick my monster hand out the door and (gently) frighten as many children as I can. It will be dark when they start arriving at my house, and lights from the street lamps will create eerie shadows of all the costumed creatures running down the block. The leaves will be whirling wildly, falling in swirling piles just meant for a young monster to stomp through as he hoots and howls, trying to scare away all the terrors of the Halloween night.

But I will miss seeing that old goblin and the tramp. How can they be too "grown up" for all this when I'm not? I know they'll help me dispense the treats, and then maybe, just maybe, the two of them will slip out of the house and take a walk in the night, kick up a few leaf piles, and relive their own special Halloween past.

Good Housekeeping — October 1986

DELIVERING THE LOCAL PAPER TURNS OUT TO BE MOM'S JOB, TOO

Dear reader, are you home right now, reading the latest edition of the local Gannett newspaper? How did you paper arrive? Were you fortunate to have it delivered?

Just look outside. Is it raining? Snowing? Or only freezing cold?

That sentimental image of a freckle-faced newsboy bicycling down Main Street on a sunny spring day, tossing his papers right and left at a regular, well-practiced pace, doesn't apply to Westchester NY in winter.

He's out there, all right, slogging through snow drifts, and battling the winds. Like his government-employed counterpart—the mail carrier—neither snow, nor rain, nor heat, nor gloom of night stays this courier from the swift completion of his appointed rounds.

No matter, you think. After all, he's getting paid for his labors, and a heavy load builds character, right?

Sure, he's getting paid, but considering the job's complexity, he's worth every penny he gets. As the parent of a newsboy, I know—all too well.

When they ask a young person if he wants to be a newspaper carrier, they ought to ask the kid's parents too.

Even though parents are paying customers who deserve equal service, they can receive second-class treatment at times. They're the ones who get soiled or torn copies ("I can't give this to my customers, Mom, so you take it.") If the order is short, parents wait for the second delivery. They help the carrier make change and figure out his bill. And if it's 9:30 at night, and the newsboy knows it's the only time he can catch the Skinflints, who owe him for four weeks' service, his parents are the ones who drive him to the Skinflints' home.

Parents are also useful for taking papers in from the street on days when it looks like rain and school doesn't let out for another hour. They're up early on Sunday mornings to drive the newsboy on his route, when the Sunday papers are too thick to fit in his bag or on the back rack of his bike.

And then comes the ultimate assistance—the day the newsboy comes home from school with a fever and there's no one to deliver the papers except good old Mom.

I knew when I enlisted in parenthood I'd be called upon to face many exciting challenges—including 3 a.m. feedings, nursery school car pools, elementary school concerts, broken bones, and chicken pox—but I never expected to be out in 5-degree weather with a day-glo orange and white canvas bag advertising GANNETT WESTCHESTER ROCKLAND digging into my shoulder and across my chest. I never thought I would grow up to be a newsboy.

I set out on a frigid January afternoon, and quickly learned how oblivious some folks are about mail carriers, delivery people, and other service persons who come to their houses. It's one thing when an elderly woman who lives alone doesn't shovel her walk right after a snow storm, but a family with five strong kids?

Hurrah! Two customers are away on vacation. They're lucky to be away from this weather, and I'm lucky, too. That's two fewer houses on my route, one which has a full flight of steps out front.

My neighborhood is filled with good houses and bad houses. The good houses have unobstructed front lawns you can cross on the bias. The bad houses have high fences or hedges all around, forcing you to enter and leave on the same path.

Lips chapped, cheeks stinging, and eyelids freezing together, I wonder why children don't dress Mommies as warmly as Mommies dress children. Why didn't I borrow my son's woolen hat/mask that covers his whole face?

Hey! A neighbor is driving by. Are you going toward Ridgeway? I could use a lift. But she doesn't hear me. Probably because she doesn't believe it's me. I've become the invisible newsboy.

I make it home in forty minutes, frozen-faced and exhausted. "Thanks Mom!" my son says. "I really appreciated this." Then, having learned that everything in this business boils down to cash, he asks, "Do you want me to pay you?"

"Oh no, I replied. "You don' t have to pay me. Just remember!

Gannett News — February 1, 1981

YOU'RE DRIVING
ME CRAZY

The day my son, Edward, turns sixteen he dashes off to the motor vehicle bureau and takes his learner's permit test. Passing it is easy; he has memorized the entire manual. The next morning, the sky is still pink with dawn but he's ready for his first lesson.

Faster than you can say, "Right turn on red," I'm gulping down orange juice and grabbing a piece of toast as he ushers me out the back door and into our car. I guess I should feel happy; when's the last time he asked me to go anywhere with him?

"You know, Mom," Edward says, turning on the engine. "If we do this every day, I'll have my license in no time."

No time. Who wants that? I'm still worn out from the first sixteen years. With this kid, I didn't have much opportunity to rest. When Edward was a baby, he hated to sleep. Night after night, he jumped around in his crib, singing merrily and asking me to play. I had a few peaceful years after he started school, although we did have to deal with middle-of-the-night monsters in the closet and goblins under the bed. But at least I knew where my son was. Now I just know there will be no sleeping again as I lie awake waiting for him to drive home in our car.

"Nice job," I say, as he steers us by two double-parked cars. "You know, driving isn't much fun when you get used to it. I probably spend half my day going back and forth to my office, chauffeuring you and your brother, going to the market, the drug store...."

"It'll be a blast!" he crows.

That's what I'm afraid of. But there is a bright side—a new camaraderie has formed between Edward and his younger brother, Peter, who knows it's in his best interests to see his big brother get his license fast.

Recently, Edward's friend Jeff, who has a driver's license, offered to drive Edward and a few buddies to the beach after school.

"It's twenty-five miles away!" I protested.

"Don't worry, Mom," Edward said. "Jeff's had his license for twelve days already. We've got maps. We'll be OK."

"But by the time you get there, you'll have to turn around and come back."

"It doesn't matter," he explained. His face glowed with excitement. "We'll be able to drive there, Mom. All by ourselves."

Then we heard Peter's voice from the next room, reciting what I call The Moses Refrain: "Let him go. Let him go."

"So now you're defending your brother?" I asked. "Not that it's not a good thing. But why now? And why this?"

"Why now?" was simple. Now was when Edward was learning to drive.

"Why this?" was simple, too. Peter knew that every privilege his brother received would eventually come his way.

The Moses Refrain has become quite popular in our house. Whenever one son asks if he can stay out late, go downtown, attend a party or do anything else I'm worried about, the other son says, "Let him go."

"Is this preoccupation with driving a male phenomenon?" I wonder, gripping the car door handle as we round a curve. Most neighborhood girls I know have little interest in learning to drive, and those who do rarely venture farther than the local mall. But as soon as every boy hits the big ONE-SIX he's out the door and down to the M.V.B.

What is this macho mania? Is it about spark plugs, axle grease, and pumping your own gas, or the ability to drive with one hand on the wheel and other hand slipping tapes into the cassette player? Why do men have this need to go off and see the world even if they're not sure where it is or why they're going? How can my teenage son forget his lunch bag, gym shorts and French book, but never his next appointment for a driving lesson?

"It's hormones," says my friend. "It goes back to nursery school. Remember how the boys always made a beeline for the cars and trucks, and the girls sat down and had tea parties?"

"Not my sons," I countered. "They played with all kinds of toys. Sure, they had cars and trucks, but they also had dolls and stuffed animals."

"And what did they do with those dolls and stuffed animals? Did they dress them up and hold tea parties?"

"Actually, come to think of it, they put them into the cars and trucks—or threw them on the toy roadways and drove over them. I give up!"

"OK," I tell Edward now. "Let's head back to the house. After you have some breakfast, I'll drive you to school."

"Forget breakfast," he answers. "I'll eat an early lunch. If we keep driving, we'll have time to practice parallel parking and three-point turns."

In less than four weeks, he's ready for his road test. Wearing his lucky shirt, lucky pants and lucky baseball cap, he passes. This is no surprise.

"Gotta go," he announces later, at home, after heartily consuming a pint of ice cream in celebration. He bolts from the kitchen table and casually lifts the car keys from the hook by the door, as if he's been doing it for years.

"Be home by dinner," I say. "And be careful, too," I add softly. I'm sure I'll be saying this countless times.

Opening the door, Edward looks at me and grins. "See you later, Mom!" Then he pauses. "Oh, is there anything you need? I'll be passing the cleaners, the deli.... If you want, I can pick up Peter at soccer practice."

Oh happy day! "Sweetheart," I croon, "Come here for a great big hug!"

Westchester Family — July 2001

RAKING DAD
OVER THE COALS

A snazzy new outdoor grill is being promoted this year. It has spacious ceramic countertops, a sink with running water, a refrigerator, rotisserie, six burners and a grill. I've heard that men are lining up to buy them; the luckiest will get theirs this Father's Day weekend.

It sounds like a kitchen to me.

Why is it that guys who wouldn't be caught dead at the kitchen stove revel in cooking outdoors? The only indoor appliance with which they are familiar is the refrigerator, although some also have nodding acquaintances with popcorn makers and coffee pots. Even the thought of putting on an apron sends them into apoplexy unless the apron proclaims the wearer is a "natural born griller," deft with supersized tongs and weighty spatulas.

Twice in twenty years, my husband, Ken, has cooked dinner indoors for our family. He whipped up a delicious Asian chicken with peanuts with great enthusiasm and pride, as if he had just figured out the reason we owned cooking pans and knives. Like a samurai let loose in a trendy steakhouse, he chopped, he sliced, he pared, he minced. Then he spooned his creation into a sizzling pan, stir-fried it and *voilà*!

"Come on downstairs and see Dad making dinner," I hollered to our sons. At last, a role model for them, and the confirmation that a tough man could cook a tender meal.

Alas, my joy was short-lived. After Ken had mastered the recipe by preparing the dish a second time, he moved on to other things. But they didn't involve cooking. I tried everything, including a "world's greatest dad" apron, to induce him to help with the daily chore of making meals, but nothing worked. Once again, Ken showed up in the kitchen only when food was on the table.

I brought him to other homes, where men cooked all the time. I suggested exotic cooking classes. No dice. Nothing could induce him to take up cooking regularly. I asked him, did he want to end up like Great-Uncle Harry, reduced to living off leftovers from restaurants after his wife died because he never learned how to cook?

"I do cook," said Ken, "in the summer, and out of doors."

That's true, but fall comes early in our neck of the woods, and many months pass before my husband wields his tongs again. And sometimes, on cold winter days when I feel like I've spent the entire day in the kitchen, when I feel like bellyaching about all the meals I've prepared and wish that Ken did some of the cooking, I have to remind myself of all the good things he does, especially tasks I hate to do: folding laundry; cleaning the bathrooms; killing bugs and disposing of them; filling up our car's gas tank at self-service stations; paying the bills and (this is a big one) balancing our checkbook; and putting up with some of my relatives, like Great-Uncle Harry.

In addition to what might be called manly chores, Ken also snips my bangs nice and straight when I don't have time to go to the hairdresser, and he gets down on his knees to pin up my uneven skirt hems so I can stitch them.

So this year, I've decided not just to accept Ken's culinary limitations, but to embrace them. After all, he's a great husband and a great dad. This Father's Day, I'm enhancing Ken's grill with a wok, a smoker and a neat pair of "grill or be grilled" oven mitts. It's not that snazzy new grill with the sink and the refrigerator, but it's a start.

Still, I can't help thinking, why should his joy flipping burgers, toasting marshmallows, barbecuing chicken and skewering kabobs of meat and vegetables be just a seasonal affair? If only there were a way to enclose his cooking area, so that he could use it year-round. We could put four walls around it, a couple of windows and a doorway linking it to the rest of the house.

But that would be a kitchen, wouldn't it?

The New York Times — June 18, 2006

LEAVING HOME

Upstairs, my son is typing. I hear the erratic taps of Edward's fingers hitting the keys. He types steadily for about two minutes, and then there's a long pause. He resumes briefly... then a long pause. He is typing his college applications. Just writing these words... astonishes me. How can it be? My blue-eyed baby boy, recently wrapped in a receiving blanket, has suddenly become 17-years old and is making plans to leave home. Starting next September, he will be living somewhere else, coming home for vacations and visits, but never coming home again for good.

I know it's the "Way of the World"—children grow up and go off, and we are glad for it. But mixed with my feelings of pride and satisfaction are strong and unsteadying emotions.

Letting go is never easy, whether it's sending your child on his first solo walk to a friend's house down the block, or watching him drive off in the family car for the first time, and knowing you won't relax until he's back. Throughout the years when my son was growing up, I gave him more and more freedom. Now, I feel like pulling him back... before I must let him go for good. Soon, he will be leaving for college. We will celebrate and send him off with parties and farewell blessings, but we won't be there when he arrives. I wish I could see what lies ahead for him, as if there were a haze on the future that I could wipe, like the mist on a steamy bathroom mirror. And I wonder, what I have I done or not done for my son, to help him prepare for this time?

I think of Janus, the ancient Roman deity with two faces, one looking forward and one looking back. I, too, am confronted with beginnings and endings, and realize they are not opposites, but subtly connected parts in the patterns of our lives. No door closes, my grandmother liked to say, without another one opening, full of new hopes, dreams, and expectations. And now as we approach the last season Edward will live at home and go to school, my thoughts turn back to his first school year, when kindergarten began.

The first weeks, I walked to school with him. We walked down our street, turned the corner, and walked to the next corner where Officer Joe, the crossing policeman, steered the neighborhood children safely across a busy, four-way intersection. School was on the other side.

Officer Joe stood in the middle of the intersection and held up traffic for Edward and me. Then, beckoning with his white-gloved hand and with a smile, he said, "Take your time, sport, no need to hurry." But Edward ran anyway, knapsack bouncing on his back.

After I stopped going with him, however, my son was reluctant to walk to school alone. He would sit on our front stoop, his jacket neatly zipped, and wait for Michael, his neighborhood friend, to come along. Michael was another five-year old who probably had his own panicky moments making it from his house to ours. He usually toodled along in a couple of minutes, and then the two boys would dash off together down the street.

They didn't walk home together all the time. Some days, their classes were dismissed a few minutes apart, and they'd come back separately. Other times, they'd wait for each other, or they'd tag along with the older children who occasionally "permitted" them to do so. Coming home was easy; it was the leaving that was difficult.

One morning, Michael's mother called, saying Michael was sick. Edward was already standing by the front door. I was busy getting his younger brother ready for nursery school, and couldn't leave the house. Could Edward get to school by himself? "You've walked to school many times," I reminded Edward. "Today will be easy, too. Just go to the corner and you'll see Officer Joe. Once you reach him, you're almost there." And then I added, "Watch Officer Joe and he'll tell you when it's safe to cross."

So Edward went off, first walking slowly, then racing to the corner. Soon, he got to school on his own. Later that day, he was brimming with pride when he returned home. "When I got to Officer Joe, he said he was very glad to see me.... And all by myself. Then he told me I wasn't really by myself."

"You weren't? Why not?" I asked.

"Because I've got him!" Edward laughed. "I've got him at the corner!"

Officer Joe was Edward's connector, his "way station" on the trip to school. He also was Edward's protector, a link between home and the outside world. And although Joe occasionally gave Edward and the other children spent shells from his gun (collected during a night hunting "coons and skunks,") he was a consistently kind and comforting person who helped my son manage on his own.

The walks to kindergarten happened a dozen years ago. These days, Edward leaves the house, day or night, with scarcely a backward glance. "Call us, if you have trouble with the car or anything else," my husband and I offer. "I'll be fine," Edward answers. Some days, that's all I need to hear. But other times, when the weather is bad, or he's going away for the weekend, visiting kids I barely know whose parents may or may not be there, I can't help adding, "Be careful, and have fun—in that order." And I remind him, never hesitate, out of false pride or stubbornness, to admit you need help if you do, because we'll always be there for you if you need us.

There won't be an Officer Joe for my son at college. There will be no one—but himself—to tell him when things are "safe." No one—but himself—on whom he can rely. Have I sufficiently helped him prepare for the future and for the inevitable reality of his leaving home? Does any parent ever know for sure?

When Edward was a young child, we were building a family. Now we are letting it go. We'll be together again, but it will be different. He will come home, but too many private and separate experiences will have occurred... for us to be a major part of his life anymore. He will be different, and we will be different, too.

I haven't heard any typing now for quite a while. I'm going upstairs, to ask if I may see the progress being made. What is he writing to the college admissions committees? What will they think when they read his personal essay? Outsiders know him only for what he is now, not for what he was. I wish I could tell them, but it's not my place. Not long ago, I offered to intervene for Edward at school and speak with a teacher whom I felt was unjust. "Please stay out of it, Mom," he insisted "You can't rescue me anymore."

"You're right," I answered, stretching up to kiss him. Feeling the soft bristles on his cheek made this kiss sweeter, somehow, than those I used to enjoy when his skin was smooth and downy. He must manage on his own now, and that—I want to tell him—is scary. And asking myself "is he ready?" is irrelevant. The future is now, ready or not.

Working Mother — November 1986

ROCK-AND-ROLL
IS A FUNDAMENTAL

Something unexpected happened to me on my way to an empty nest. I knew I'd miss a lot of things when my sons left for college. But I never thought I'd miss their music.

I had expected to miss the rest of the ruckus, especially during the most recent years, with two teen-agers in the house. In fact, I had become fairly used to the loud bang of doors slamming, boys vaulting up and down stairs, cars screeching in and out of my driveway and telephones ringing late at night.

But recently, I've been feeling sad and lonely, bereft of other sounds I never thought I'd long to hear—the loud pulsing pounding of drums, the throbbing booms of synthesizers, the twang of guitar strings and the thunder of rock music slamming out of oversized speakers. Everything electrified. Everything larger than life.

I'm not a big rock music fan. The first time my sons went to a real rock concert, I went with them, to see for myself how horrible the scene really was. And it wasn't half bad, except for the deafening volume of the music, which I managed to bring down to a tolerable level by pushing wax stopples into my ears.

I watched my sons and hundreds of other kids clapping, dancing and shouting to the music. Long gone were the days of *Hush Little Baby* and *Where Is Thumkin?*. They have been replaced by the passion of ancient, pulse-like poundings and songs with titles like *Heart Too Hot to Hold* and *I'll Sleep When I'm Dead.*

Some people condemn rock music, saying it leads to loose morals, wild sex and heavy drugs. But it didn't happen that way in my house. Music was as fundamental to my sons' lives as putting on shoes. They rarely did anything without music playing nearby.

Peter would flip the switch on the radio in the kitchen and scramble his eggs in concert to the beat. I watched him click the fork tines against the sides of a metal mixing bowl, building up to a rapid staccato until he poured the eggs into a sizzling pan, swished them around, scooped them out, and deftly deposited the eggs on his breakfast plate.

Upstairs, Edward worked out on a rowing machine, his strong arms moving back and forth, back and forth and his head going up and down in steady rhythms that matched almost magically the music blasting from his stereo.

Both sons are now at college—gone for months, although not quite gone for good. I miss them and I miss their music. "Listen to me, listen to me," their music would demand. Hear the power and explosions and hear the sheer loud rocketing sensations of it all. Hear the joy of our lives, it was telling me. This is our affirmation that we are really here. And that we are really alive.

The New York Times — April 23, 1989

MY HOUSE IS FILLED WITH PHOTOGRAPHS

My stepfather stands with my three-year-old son by the edge of a blue-green lake. Their backs are toward the camera, and they are holding hands. Whenever I look at this family photograph, what I sense most, in their reaching toward each other, is the love between them, and the comforting bond between generations. And now, many years later, after my stepfather has died and my son has left for college, the sweet poignancy of the picture is even more precious.

My house is filled with photographs. They cover the walls of my kitchen, dining room and den. There are pictures of my sons, showing the subtle but steady changes in their development as they grow into young men literally before my eyes. There are pictures of my parents, and of my husband and me.

Recently, I have begun to feel like Janus, the ancient Roman deity with two faces—one looking forward and one looking back. I look at my family's photographs and see our entire history, starting with my wedding, continuing through the births of both sons, buying a home, family gatherings and family vacations. And I wonder, do we really need photographs to remind us of special moments? Couldn't we remember those times just as well without pictures, because the memories are embedded in our hearts?

When my sons were little, they loved to pose for the camera. They waved, danced, climbed trees, batted balls, hung upside down from the jungle gym—anything for a picture. But when the boys reached adolescence, photograph-taking changed into something they barely tolerated. Their bodies were growing at haphazard speeds. Their voices cracked, and their smooth cheeks grew stubbly. Reluctantly, they stood with us or their grandparents at birthday celebrations and other occasions, and smiled weakly at the camera for as short a time as possible. They not only hated to pose for pictures, but avoided looking at them afterward. They squirmed with embarrassment when friends noticed all the snapshots we kept on display.

I am the chronicler of all our photographs. Although my husband takes most of the pictures, I select those to be framed and I arrange the rest of them in albums. This task is not always pleasurable, especially when the envelopes of prints pile up on the kitchen counter, urging me to save the photos before they are ruined or (G-d forbid) lost. But once the pictures are taken and have been developed, I can't ever throw them out.

The process of saving and arranging the photos becomes addictive, and, as the shelves that hold our albums become more and more filled, I wonder what will become of them. Will anyone look at these photos in future years? Will my sons take them out and look at them? If they do, what will they think of us and of themselves?

Four years ago, on a bright August afternoon that was to be the last day I would ever see my stepfather alive, I took some snapshots of him with my husband as they fished together on a lake near our vacation house.

As my sons and I sat on the shore and watched them row away, I picked up the camera and photographed the beautiful lake, surrounded by summer-heavy green trees, and the two men I loved, who were gradually growing smaller until all I could see were my stepfather's red shirt, my husband's green shirt, and the tan and blue caps on their heads.

Within a week, the photos became priceless to us, and I wept when I pasted them into our album.

I wept again, not long ago, when I saw my younger son looking at those photos. It was a few days before he left for college. He had taken down all our albums from the bookshelves in the den, and spread them out before him on the carpeted floor. It had been a very long time since I'd seen him doing this. Once he stopped wanting to pose for pictures, he had seemed to lose interest in looking at them. But now he was on the verge of leaving home. This was his special time to look ahead and look back.

I stood for a moment in the hallway by the den, and I then I tiptoed away. I didn't take a photo of my son that afternoon, but I will remember how he looked for as long as I live. Some pictures, I learned, don't have to be taken with a camera.

Working Mother — July 1990

ONE FAMILY'S BACK PAGES

Eva and her mother, Sarah ca. 1949

BRANCHES
OF THE FAMILY

Soon after my relatives learned that I was doing research into family history, they began making comments and offering advice. Reactions ranged from cool disinterest—"Who cares?" to finger wagging admonitions: "Leave things alone, everything's fine as it is," to assistance (sort of)—"If you want to know what really happened, just ask me," to ominous portents, offered with a "tsk:" "Why go looking for trouble? You never can tell what you might find out."

Amateur genealogists are busy these days. They're poring over old documents and photographs, and digging through archives, library records, and family tree websites. Male researchers focus, primarily, on the facts: dates of birth, marriages, and death. The women are also looking for the stories: What happened when so-and-so left the old country and headed for America? Who sponsored her? What made her go? Why did those brothers and sisters stop talking to each other? What made that marriage end?

Like me, the female researchers probably spent their girlhoods listening to grownups gossip at the dinner table. Afterwards, the men continued talking as they eased themselves into living room chairs, while the women cleaned up in the kitchen, clucking over their progeny's achievements and sighing heavily over someone's bad health or bad luck (it usually was both.)

Since 1990, the number of Jews researching their roots has grown ten-fold, according to Gary Mokotoff, publisher of <u>Avotaynu, the International Review of Jewish Genealogy</u>. Web site portals, such as *www.jewishgen.org* receive about one million "hits" a month, and that's not counting thousands of other sites maintained by smaller organizations and private families.

And, in perhaps, the biggest boon of all, the first phase of a database information center about our ancestors' arrivals at Ellis Island was opened in April, 2001 at Ellis Island's American Family Immigration Center.

Experts in the field warn that you can't find everything on the Web. "Most research is still done using original documents and archival records on microfilm," says Renee Steinig, past president of The Jewish Genealogy Society of Long Island.

I know what she means. This year, I've been spending long hours studying microfilmed indexes, ship manifests, naturalization papers, city directories, and census reports at New York City's Municipal Archives, and the National Archives in Lower Manhattan. The offices are crowded with other neophyte genealogists. We help each other with useful tips, rejoice in our discoveries, and commiserate over unavoidable frustrations.

For the most part, we agree, there are no secrets in families—just things that no one wants to talk about.

Misrepresentations—such as claiming to be a native-born American—are now only charming fabrications. Two of my grandparents promulgated this falsehood, but it's easy to understand why. My maternal grandmother emigrated when she was 5-years-old and was fervently proud to speak

English without an accent, unlike "greenhorns who just got off the boat." By the time I was born, about fifty years after she skipped off the dock at Ellis Island, she probably had forgotten that her story was a lie.

In my own quest for ancestral connections, I have located a third cousin through a Jewish genealogy website, after he posted a query about his great-grandmother's shtetl, and we determined that she was my great-great aunt.

We're interviewing elderly relatives near and far, and we are fascinated by the similarities of their recollections. "G," one of my grandfather's brothers who moved to Philadelphia and ran a hardware store, is remembered by three distant relatives as "a sweetheart," "a darling man," and "the nicest of them all." But "C," another brother's second wife, was "a terrible nag," so horrible that "she practically threw the children from his first marriage out of the house." "I" was "no angel," but his wife was "snobbish" and "egocentric," someone who "always expected others to wait on her." Even worse, she was "an evil scold who purposely made trouble between her own children and drove them apart." Oh dear.

We researchers fill in the blanks in our family trees, noting each person's vital statistics. As we write down our own names and those of our children, we can't help noticing the tiny dash alongside our dates of birth. Someday, another date will be recorded, and all that may remain will be our own good names. And sometimes, it may all boil down to one short phrase.

May we all be remembered as "sweet hearts."

The Jewish Week of New York — April 12, 2002

HOW WE "REMEMBER THE DAY"

It wasn't until after I located the April 1895 immigration papers and ship's manifest for my great grandmother Chaya Lempert and her four children that I determined that they had arrived in America *Erev Pesach.*

I can't imagine that Chaya was dusting her shelves with a feather before Passover that year, but maybe the Lemperts attended someone's Seder—possibly in the Lower East Side building where my great grandfather Isaac had already set up their home. My grandmother Etta would have been 5-years-old.

Many immigrants did share Old World stories with their families, but in mine, the past was past and rarely talked about. Long after Etta had died, I figured out that her unabashed pride in being a native-born American was a fabrication. She never let on that she had been born in a faraway Galician shtetl instead of New York City. But if she had told us, maybe she would have said, "We landed at Ellis Island right before the first night of Passover. And like the ancient Israelites long ago, we had crossed the sea to a land of freedom."

Those of us with few stories of family history still want to enrich our Seders (and our lives) with meaningful pieces of the past. Now that my husband and I have young grandchildren at our table, we've added ways to make our Seder meaningful to them.

We have made our own "Red Sea," a rectangular piece of blue paper with hand-drawn waves, and taped it to the foyer floor. Everyone who enters our house must "cross" it. We've also helped the youngsters write and assemble their own *Haggadot*.

Accompanying the text is a photo of Chaya, Isaac, Etta and her siblings, taken soon after they had settled in New York. There also are pictures of scenes from Exodus, which the children enhance with holiday stickers and original art. This year, they are choosing their "favorite" plagues in advance, and they will tell us stories about them.

After that, at the appropriate time in our service, Grandpa leaves the room and returns wearing a magnificent golden Pharaoh hat. Then he sits down solemnly and says he is waiting for Moses. "Where is he?" the parents ask. Then, "Who wants to be Moses?" "I do!" "I do!" the children clamor. Colorful shawls are wrapped around their shoulders, and one by one, they approach Grandpa-Pharaoh.

"Let my people go!" each Moses demands, and threatens him with plagues if he refuses. At first, Grandpa-Pharaoh says, "NO!" "NO!" "NO!" After what seems like a thousand "NOs," the tyrant relents.

"Freedom!" all the Moseses cheer, and they run for the Red Sea in the foyer. That's when Grandpa-Pharaoh changes his mind. He hurries after them, falls down, flounders in the Red Sea, and "drowns." What else can the Israelites do now, but fall on top of him and gently pummel him with hugs and giggly kisses?

Remember this day, when you went out of Egypt!

The Jewish Week of New York — Spring 2010

FINDING FAMILY, AND MAKING PEACE

" Don't you know about *'le scandale?'* asked a distant cousin I recently met.

"Only bits and pieces," I replied. No one ever fully explained why my grandparents' marriage ended sixty-five years ago. How could my mother's father—my grandfather, Aaron—a "good provider" who had given his family everything, lose touch with his children, and spend the last thirty years of his life alone? How could my grandmother, who showered me with unconditional love and untiring devotion, who dedicated all her energies to the mundane and fatiguing chores that go with raising two grandchildren and running a home, be so angry with her husband that she left him and refused to ever speak of him again?

I saw Aaron briefly, once or twice, when I was little, and never knew other members of his family. Divorces, separations, and ancient disputes over money had scattered the descendants of my immigrant relations. Pockets of relatives remained loving and close, but our family tree had many severed branches. Now, my interest in genealogy prodded me to put the names on faces in withered photographs, and make sense of the reasons things had fallen apart. My grown children had married, and my research would also enable them to understand their family histories.

My distant and elderly cousin admitted that she knew few details. "Back then, your grandparents' breakup was a very big topic, and created a serious rift within our family. People took sides, and stopped talking to everyone on the 'other side.'"

In July 1901, my grandfather Aaron immigrated to America from Zbarazh, which is now part of Ukraine. He was 17, and loaded with gumption.

Aaron embarked on a ship from Antwerp, sailed to New York and settled on the Lower East Side, where he worked briefly in a factory. A year or so later, he declared that he would work for no one again, and established his own successful contracting business.

Over the next decades, he bought ship passages to America for his widowed father, brothers and sisters. Only one brother remained in Europe, and he would barely survive the horrors of the Holocaust.

By the time Aaron married my grandmother in 1911, he was a prosperous entrepreneur with his own horse and carriage. His wealth grew in the 1920s, and though he wished for a son to "say *Kaddish* when I die," his three daughters lacked for nothing. They were educated and indulged, until the long years of the Great Depression wore down my grandparents' love for each other, and wiped out their wealth.

The final blow came when Aaron wrestled control from my grandmother of their last piece of property, which was her only means of support. After terrible battles, she left him in 1938. The grown daughters remained close to their mother, but—as often happens in splintered families—

issues of loyalty and taking sides prevented them from maintaining relationships with their father, too.

The raging hostilities made Aaron's siblings uncomfortable, and they also drifted away.

In 1945, my father and my mother separated. I was a baby when she, my older brother and I moved into my grandmother's apartment, and stayed there for the rest of my childhood. My mother found a job to support us, and my grandmother took care of us. She was loving, generous, and incredibly kind, but just mentioning Aaron's name made her blood boil.

Aaron outlived all his siblings and his wife, and died in a nursing home in 1967, at the age of 84. I didn't know this until recently, when I obtained a copy of his death certificate. That's when I realized that it was time to find Aaron. What happened to my grandparents should not have spun out to future generations. I cannot feel anger toward a man I never knew, even though he deeply wounded the woman who loved me so much.

On a hot summer day, my son and I went to an old Jewish cemetery in Queens, and visited Aaron's grave for the first time. We were relieved to see that he was buried beside siblings. But while his brothers' headstones affirm, "husband, father, grandfather," his simply says, "May his soul rest in peace."

I thought about my grandmother, and felt the old, heart-wrenching ache that that still grips me whenever I remember her. She was the one who stroked my hair and calmed my fears on the darkest nights. She was the one who tried to teach me patience, and told me things would get better whenever they were bad. I wished that I could tell her—what Aaron did was terrible. You were right to be furious, but you had your family for the rest of your life. Look what it cost him. It cost him everything.

Anger dies away, and old hurts melt with the passage of the years. Little by little, with keen satisfaction, I am locating members of Aaron's family and mine. One gave me a photo of Aaron, and said he never got over the breakup. That afternoon in the cemetery, 101 years after Aaron arrived in America, and thirty-four years after he died, his great-grandson and I said *Kaddish* for him.

The Jewish Week of New York — December 19, 2003

FINDING EVA

In New York, it was a Sunday morning in August, 1999. In Tel Aviv, it was afternoon. I took a deep breath, picked up the telephone, and dialed fourteen numbers.

"*Shalom*?" said an elderly woman.

"*Shalom*," I replied. "And hello. I am looking for Eva Hessing. Are you Eva?"

"Yes." She spoke English well, but her voice sounded guarded and cautious: "Who are you?"

Another deep breath, and I began, "I am the granddaughter of Aaron Bell, calling from New York," I said. "I want to thank you for taking care of my grandfather years ago, before he died."

Silence. Eva paused. Then: "Aaron? You are Uncle Aaron's granddaughter?" She stopped again; was she also holding her breath? She resumed, speaking slowly and deliberately." If you are calling me about my great-uncle Aaron, then there is justice in heaven, after all. And I am happy to speak to you," she said.

"Even if that was all you did, Susan, that phone call to thank Eva was enough," my rabbi said recently, when I described the event to her. "The fact that you called surely meant a lot to Eva. It was a call she would never forget."

I, too, would never forget the call. Quickly, Eva concluded that we were second cousins, since our grandfathers had been brothers in Zbarazh, their hometown in Galicia, although her grandfather Jacob had been much older than Aaron.

The brothers weren't alike; possibly, they never had been. Even before 1901, when Aaron came to America, Jacob had moved permanently to Budapest. Deeply religious, he married twice, fathered eleven children, and became president of the Kaczinsky Street synagogue. In New York, Aaron became a successful businessman, entrenched in a secular world and life, and eventually paid for the passage of all his other siblings to the New World.

On the phone that first day, Eva's next question to me was stunning: "Do you know that you are calling me on the *Yahrzeit* of Aaron's death?"

No, I didn't know, although I knew that Aaron had died in August. But Eva was correct. Thirty-two years ago, my grandfather had died *Erev Tisha b'Av*, which was now. She had been lighting candles in his memory ever since. His siblings had died before him, and his children never mentioned him. For years, Eva had been remembering a long-forgotten man. Now, genealogical research had driven me to find this woman who had called herself his "Next of Kin" on his death certificate.

"There is a photograph of him on my bureau, and I am looking at it now," she said. "Come to Tel Aviv. I would love to meet you and we will talk and talk. You can stay with me, your only expense will be your airfare."

Did finding Eva just happen, or was it meant to be? Had it simply been chance that I had called her on the anniversary of Aaron's death? The concurrence of these events was remarkable.

"I do believe that our ancestors... want to be found!" writes genealogist Henry Z. Jones, Jr. in his book, <u>Psychic Roots: Serendipity and Intuition in Genealogy</u>. Jones contends that unseen forces are at work when we actively search for something, and that "serendipitous and intuitive events do indeed influence our research."

Swiss analytical psychologist Carl Jung said "meaningful coincidences" must be valued and examined, and not simply taken for granted. Cues are always there, but usually, we don't notice them unless we sense we are in the right place, at the right time."

I'm a big believer in happenstance, especially when I pursue family tree research. When I began my work, all I expected was to fill in gaps of missing information. I had not yet realized that genealogy helps you connect to your heritage; sometimes you're not just writing down birth and death dates, you're also reuniting dispersed families torn apart by wars, geography or breakdowns in family ties due to all kinds of reasons.

I found Eva because I was looking for Aaron, whom I had met only once or twice when I was very young. By then, my grandmother had left him and ended their marriage, and their children had drifted away, too. Many years later, I applied for a copy of his death certificate, and what I learned inspired me to dig deeply into family history, search for missing relatives, fly to Israel, eastern Europe, and Ukraine. Eva had signed the death certificate, but no one knew who she was. For months, I contacted all the relatives I knew and all the relatives they knew.

Metaphorically leapfrogging across domestic and international borders, I phoned, wrote letters, and sent emails asking, "Do you know Eva Hessing?" Respondents kept saying no.

At the same time, I plowed through microfilm rolls at Federal Archives offices, and almost disregarded the 1901 ship manifest of a young man with my grandfather's last name, Bialazurker (before it was Anglicized), until I sounded out the first: "Uren," and realized it was, indeed, a misspelling of "Aaron."

Online, through *www.jewishgen.org*, I also discovered a faraway third cousin whose great-grandmother had been Aaron's aunt back in Galicia.

Finally, a previously unknown relative whom I had queried asked his elderly mother who said, "Try Lici, in Toronto. She's not a blood relative, but more like a 'waving relative.'" I sent Lici an email introducing myself, and asking my perpetual question. A week later, she responded: "Your grandfather's caretaker was indeed Eva, who now lives in Tel Aviv. She's past 80, widowed and childless, and she will fall in love with you immediately as she loves to tell old family tales."

Finding Eva was the start of peeling the onion of my family's world before most of my relatives came to America. The stories she would tell were not only about my grandfather, but also were powerful recollections about how she survived the Holocaust in Hungary and World War II... and how other family members did not. You can't investigate 20th century Jewish history without colliding with the Holocaust. Even if I thought everyone in my family was "here," in the United States, the Holocaust had hacked off branches of my family tree.

Four months after I called Eva, my husband, Ken, and I flew to Tel Aviv to meet her for the first time. We'd been to Israel before, and always said we were tourists when passport and immigration inspectors asked us the reason for our trip. Now, I said I was "visiting family," which made the inspector smile.

Tiny and round, as Lici had predicted, Eva opened her apartment door and greeted Ken and me with warm hugs. After a leisurely *Shabbat* dinner, she began telling us story after story....

Connecting the dots of family history happened whenever I listened to Eva. She and her younger sister, Alice, had been born in Budapest, Hungary, in 1918 and 1921. During World War II, they worked in the Resistance during the Nazi invasion in 1944, gave shelter and food to many homeless Jews, and forged life-saving identification papers and other documents for them. Eventually, Eva's stories inspired Ken and me to visit the sites she so vividly described. With her Aryan features, strawberry blonde hair, and a safe apartment under "Swedish protection," Eva and Alice took in Jews with no place to stay for short or extended periods of time. Jacob and his second wife came often, until they found sanctuary in a Swedish Red Cross hospital even though, technically, they were not ill. "But they were starving," said Eva. "All of us were.

"By December, everything was broken down. There was little food or water, no heat, no electricity... all was chaos. Some days, the only 'food' we had was salt."

Even so, Eva agreed to hide a boy named Peter, the young son of a desperate mother whose husband was a Jew. After Eva put on one of the Nazi armbands that she had made for the Underground, she brought Peter to an 18th century church run by Franciscan monks known to hide Jews in their secluded cloister. But a few days later, as the Red Army advanced toward Budapest, Eva learned that the Nazis had emptied the cloister and killed everyone they saw, including the monks.

Probably, Peter was dead, but Eva was determined to search for him. In what she would later call "my bravest act," she "rushed to the cloister, ran inside and down a long narrow corridor, turned right, came to a door, opened it and there was Peter, crying in a corner. 'No crying! We have to run,' I whispered, as I helped him into a coat. I grabbed his hand and we left, ran down the corridor and out the door to the street. Then we walked slowly, as if nothing had happened. I felt that we were invisible." Peter stayed with Eva for several months, until his mother came for him in spring, 1945.

When Ken and I went to Budapest, we searched neighborhoods for days until we found the Franciscan church on the corner of Kossuth and Ferenciek streets. Situated beside it was another building with tall, wooden doors. Did they open on a long corridor? After about ten minutes, a man unlocked the doors and disappeared down a dim passageway. Other people entered, and we followed. Turning right at the end of the hall, we saw a middle-aged monk in the sacristy. His eyes shifted unsteadily when we introduced ourselves as Jews, but a younger monk named Clement spoke English well and listened to our story about Eva and Peter. Quickly, Clement led us to a room with windows facing only an interior courtyard, safely hidden from the street. Elderly nuns had once told him that this was where Jews had been sheltered in 1944. The air was thick with ghosts.

I remembered Eva saying that most of the monks had not been "friendly" to the Jews. Now, I told Clement, "What the monks did, helping Jews, was a brave and very good thing. We came here to thank you, and to let you know that such bravery has not been forgotten." Clement smiled modestly, and promised that our gratitude would also be known.

This is just one of the stories that Eva told me. Another one can be found in the 1993 book, <u>Young People Speak: Surviving the Holocaust in Hungary</u>, edited by Susan V. Meschel and written by Hungarian-born adults who were children during the war years. They remembered "Eva the Swede," a kind woman with reddish-blond hair who worked in the underground in Budapest, gave shelter and food to many Jews, and helped them obtain lifesaving identification papers.

I'll never forget Eva's words, to me, before she slipped into dementia a year ago. It was the last time we had a meaningful conversation. "We met too late, dear Susan," she said.

"Oh, but we did meet, Eva, and hasn't it been amazing that we met at all?"

Directions Magazine of the *Jewish Week of New York* — December 2009

ONE FAMILY'S BACK PAGES

Every family has its "truths," and firmly established myths. When I was growing up, in the years after World War II, we believed—actually, we knew—that no family members had suffered directly, or been killed in the Holocaust because "everyone" had already emigrated from Europe to America.

Hadn't my grandmother come to New York with her parents and brothers in 1895? Hadn't all her aunts, uncles and cousins followed subsequently, often sleeping on two chairs pushed together in crowded but always-with-room-for-one-more Lower East Side tenement apartments?

Hadn't my grandfather Aaron left home in Galicia at 17, and sailed to America in 1901? He wasn't the eldest son but surely he was the one most determined to do well. Aaron was the first to marry and succeed financially in the *goldene medina*. He paid for the voyages of sisters and brothers who arrived with spouses and children in tow, year after year, until 1922. Even his widowed father, Moshe, had finally agreed to leave Eastern Europe, and spent his last years in a daughter's home, reading Torah every day until his death in 1933. But he was here.

So who stayed behind? No one. Or so it was thought, until I started to research my family's history, and learned that Aaron had another brother, Jacob, who never came to America. I discovered Jacob's name on the family tree of a third cousin, on a Jewish genealogy website. Jacob was the eldest child who had married and moved to Budapest around the same time his siblings had packed their bags for the New World. Eventually, he married twice, fathered eleven children,* and prospered financially, too.

Probably, the last time Aaron saw Jacob was in the early 1920s, when my grandfather made his final trip to Europe. The brothers weren't close; perhaps they never had been. Aaron was the successful businessman, entrenched in a secular world and life. Jacob was deeply religious and observant; if he didn't want to emigrate, so be it. Budapest was cosmopolitan and lively. It was too good to leave in the 1920s, and by the late 1930s it was impossible to do so. Jacob was more than 60-years-old, trapped in Budapest with most of his family. I ached to know what had happened to them.

At first, I thought that there was no one to ask, because all the old-timers had long since died. But after much circuitous investigation, I tracked down two of Jacob's granddaughters, Eva and Alice, elderly women living in Tel Aviv. Back in the 1960s, Eva had lived for a while in New York City, where she cared for her ailing great-uncle who lived alone after his wife left him. That great-uncle was my grandfather Aaron.

From 1938 to 1945, some members of Jacob's family escaped Budapest and went to Denmark and Sweden. Others hid in haylofts, hospitals or convents, or fought bravely in the underground, supplying food and arms to those in even more terrible situations. Some were captured and brutally murdered by the Nazis.

In 1944, the Swedish diplomat Raoul Wallenberg personally saved one of Jacob's sons and other Jews on trains bound for death camps by handing them life-saving Swedish passports. Jacob survived until 1945, when he suffered a fatal heart attack precipitated by news that his daughter, Margit, had died at Auschwitz after throwing herself against a high voltage electric fence.

How could Jacob's American family not know? Probably, some relatives did but no one told us because in 1937 connections were broken by my grandparents' permanent separation. Their grown children blamed their father for the troubles, and sided with their mother. They lost touch with everyone on Aaron's side of the family. Only now, more than sixty years later, have we found out what happened.

Recently, I visited Eva and Alice in Tel Aviv, and we hugged each other dearly, like the long lost relatives we are. Like many survivors, they are still recovering from their painful past. They protected each other throughout the bombings of Budapest, and they continue to sustain each other today. Eva took care of Aaron when he was old and ill, and I can't thank her enough for doing so. "He was a very dear man, with a difficult life," she says. He outlived all his brothers and sisters, and would have died alone if not for Eva. That I should find her now, after all these years, means "there is a kind of justice in heaven," she says.

When we finally part, I promise to stay in touch. After all, we're family.

The Jewish Week of New York — March 31, 2000

* Author's Note: A fuller description about finding Eva appears in another piece, "Finding Eva," published 2009. Also, in 2016, Jacob's grandson Danny, the son of Jacob's youngest daughter, Suzi, contacted me from his home in Sydney, Australia, after reading my memoir, *Because of Eva.*

HOW HUNGARIAN SISTERS OUTWITTED THE NAZIS

This month marks the 70th anniversary of the German occupation of Budapest, which began on March 19, 1944. In 2006, my husband, Ken, and I went to Budapest to see as much as possible that related to Jewish life during that horrendous time.

Sixty-two years had passed since my second cousins, Eva and Alice Eismann, had been classified as "Exceptional Jews" in June 1944 and had been given lifesaving Swedish protection and sanctuary at the address Rakoczi utca 12. Until then, they had been, literally, on the run.

As Ken and I approached the red brick apartment house, we felt exhilaration as well as trepidation. The front door was locked, so we stood nearby and waited until someone came out. Soon a woman exited; we caught the door before it shut, and entered the lobby. Harsh fluorescent lights illuminated cardboard and wooden crates jumbled in a pile on the worn stone floor. Mainly, the room was empty, but the air was thick with ghosts and the sounds of people long gone.

When I first located Eva, in 1999, I was searching for information about my late grandfather, not about his extended family. Eva had known and cared for my grandfather at the end of his life. She was 81-years-old now, widowed and childless. On the telephone her voice was lyrical and sweet.

"Come to Tel Aviv," she said. "We will talk and reminisce." Her Hungarian accent and intonation promised something more than just the facts, and I would soon learn that genealogy doesn't just help you learn the dates of births and deaths; it can repair family ties severed by wars, the Holocaust and divorce (in my case, those of my parents and grandparents).

Ken and I made plans to go.

Four months later, we arrived at Eva's apartment. Eva was pint-sized and plump. She wore a navy cotton dress, and her white hair was in a braided bun. No makeup was on her face, but her apple cheeks, green eyes and exuberant smile affirmed that in 1944, Eva had surely been a beauty. Alice, who had walked over from her nearby apartment, was slim and fashionably dressed. She wore makeup, and her tinted hair was stylishly cut.

After a delightful and bountiful meal, Ken and I gently asked the sisters how they had survived the war years in Budapest. Their story would be long, Eva cautioned, and "big, like a book." Hearing this, I asked for their permission to write down their words. Eva and Alice nodded their approval, and began by telling us about their father, Yehuda, who audaciously managed for seven years to save his wife and five children from the clutches of the Nazi "beasts."

In December 1938, Yehuda and his wife, Sarah, secured permission to take their younger children (underage minors whose names were on Yehuda's travel document) for a "holiday" to Denmark, from where they subsequently made their way to Stockholm. Eva, 20, and Alice, 16, were expected to follow, but new anti-Jewish restrictions barred them from leaving Budapest.

After that, they could not attend school or work. Although they were Hungarian born, they no longer had rights of citizenship.

"Without legitimate papers, we were always in danger, and moved around constantly," Eva said. From time to time, they lived with relatives or friends, but mainly the sisters slept in deserted buildings, shops that had closed for the day, basements or attics of sympathetic Christians, or abandoned barns and chicken coops. Sometimes they fled only moments before random police raids.

By 1944, Hungary was on the verge of falling to the Allies when the Germans invaded. In May, almost half a million Hungarian Jews were deported from the countryside and sent to Auschwitz, Mauthausen and Buchenwald.

Alice's dark Semitic features put her at great risk of capture, but Eva's fair skin and strawberry blonde hair enabled her to "pass" for a gentile. She had been in the Resistance for several years, but now her participation intensified. She stole and forged documents with false names for herself, Alice and other hidden Jews. Later, she would also work with Raoul Wallenberg, the Swedish diplomat who saved the lives of thousands of Hungarian Jews.

In June, Yehuda learned that his daughters were living in Budapest with a Swedish woman named Ellen. He went to the Astoria Hotel in Stockholm, called Ellen from a public telephone, and was comforted to hear that everyone was safe. But, Eva recalled: "After ten minutes, the phone rang again, and a stranger said he was calling from the Astoria Hotel. Ellen gave me the phone, but... it was a Gestapo officer at the Astoria Hotel *in Budapest,* which was headquarters of the Gestapo! Father's call had been overheard! The officer demanded that Alice and I be there at nine o'clock the next morning. We knew that Jews who went to the Astoria were lost and never came back." Immediately Eva called Yehuda in Stockholm, hinting that she and Alice had been found. He understood.

Fortunately, Yehuda had befriended a journalist who knew the secretary of King Gustav V. Within hours, the "stateless Hungarian Jew" was received by the king, who listened sympathetically and commanded that Swedish citizenship be granted to Yehuda's daughters at once. Early the next morning, on June 14, they stood before Per Anger, the attaché at Budapest's Swedish Legation, as he dialed Gestapo headquarters at the Astoria Hotel. "What do you want with my citizens?" he asked. "Nothing now," the officer said snidely.

Forthwith, the eternally grateful sisters moved into a third-floor apartment under Swedish protection at Rakoczi utca 12. Their apartment would be a perpetual godsend and safe harbor for 20–25 homeless Jews who slipped in, ate, slept and tiptoed out silently, lest nosy neighbors question excessive noise.

Around the corner was Sip utca 12, the local Jewish community center. Until December, when the Nazis sealed the ghetto, Eva and Alice shepherded Jewish children from the ghetto to the community center for hot food and a safe place to play in the interior courtyard.

Wallenberg arrived at the Swedish legation in Budapest in early July, around the same time that the roundups stopped. After they resumed in late summer, he began distributing *Schutz-passes* (special Swedish passports) to

Jews onboard trains heading to the death camps. German soldiers accepted the official-looking passes, and thousands of Jews were let go. "To get a *Schutz-pass*, all you had to do was show Wallenberg a document — any document," Eva said. "If you gave him a receipt for your dirty laundry, he accepted it."

By late fall, "everything was breaking down," she said. "You could go outside to buy bread and be shot to death. That happened to my dear friend, Teri." Aerial attacks drove terrified inhabitants to basement shelters repeatedly. Food supplies dwindled, and dead bodies lay in the streets. The top floors of Eva and Alice's building were bombarded; windows were shattered, and there was no electricity or heat. Water came from only one pipe in the building basement. The sisters dragged home splintered wood they found, and burned it indoors.

In early December they heard the cries of an abandoned baby outside their windows. The infant lay on the freezing pavement all night, but they couldn't save it, because Arrow Cross (Hungarian Nazi) soldiers blocked the building exits. "By morning it was dead," Alice said. We could tell she still was sad about this.

"On Sylvester night (New Year's Eve), there was great chaos in the streets," Eva said. "Germans and Arrow Cross were fighting the Russians, and our building was at the edge of two fronts. Alice and I rushed to the shelter, but this time we forgot our identification papers. About 150 people — mostly Aryans, some Jews — were crowded inside.

"Into the shelter came two Arrow Cross soldiers — young thugs with weapons, wearing heavy warm uniforms and big boots. 'Out with the Exceptions when good

Hungarian blood runs in the streets!' they yelled. 'We came for the stinking Jews with the Exceptions!' Carefully, I felt in my braided hair for two cyanide capsules I had hidden there; if necessary, Alice and I would use them now.

"As the soldiers tramped by, people presented their papers. One man said he was the son of a Jewish World War I hero and showed his father's gold medal. But the soldiers smacked him, cursed him, grabbed him by the neck, shoved him into a corner and killed him. Next, a man who had converted to Catholicism from Judaism and married a Catholic woman said that the Pope said you're not a Jew if you converted before marriage, but the soldiers dragged him into the corner and killed him, too."

Eva and Alice waited in a far corner. "Near us was an old woman and her middle-aged daughter who had a little dog, a corgi she adored. It was like her child," Eva said. "They were looking for their papers when the soldiers reached them. The dog started barking furiously. 'People are dying of hunger, and you are feeding this beast?' one of the soldiers shouted. He kicked the dog to death with his boots.

"The daughter howled, and beat the soldier. She wanted to kill him! There was great tumult until both soldiers pushed her away and said, 'Let's go!' The one who had been not as vicious turned to me and asked, 'Did you legitimate yourselves?' I knew he meant did Alice and I show him our papers. I was shaking, but I said, 'Don't you remember?' He left, and the cyanide stayed in my hair. That dog saved us. To this day, I have a fondness for corgis."

These stories and others kept spinning in my head as Ken and I stood in the silent lobby; so much had happened here, at Rakoczi utca 12, not that you could tell. But for us to be in this ordinary-looking building and know its personal history was to see Wallenberg stride across the tiled floor, to hear the stomping of soldiers' boots, and the gunfire in the basement below. We knew these things and more because Eva had told it all to us before dementia began to steal her memories.

The sisters fled Budapest in March 1945, when a sympathetic Soviet soldier secured passage for them on one of the last trains out of the city before the Iron Curtain shut the borders. The soldier had knocked forcefully on their door, Eva recalled, and said: "Hurry! The train is waiting for you now!" She sensed that he was a Jew, especially because "he kept looking at me, and looking at my *mezuza* by the door. He wanted me to see him doing this."

Six months later, she and Alice were reunited with their family in Denmark and Sweden. They lived together for a while, until Eva went to Palestine in 1948 to fight in Israel's War of Independence. Eventually she moved to New York; in 1979 she made *aliyah* and "came home" to Israel. But she never went back to Budapest.

Alice died in 2006, a few months before our trip to Budapest. Eva died in 2010, at the age of 92.

Before Ken and I left my cousins' building, I wanted to climb upstairs to see if the *mezuza* or its indentation still marked the doorway. I wanted to go down to the basement, too, but Ken was apprehensive. "We're in a country that was long under Communist rule," he said. "We must be careful not to overstep our bounds."

A middle-aged man walked into the building. He approached us slowly, and when I gestured that we didn't speak Hungarian, he nodded and asked, in broken English, who we were, and what did we want.

I explained that we were curious to see where my cousins lived long ago. "Do you know the building's history?" I asked. "Well, I've lived here thirty years," he said. I paused: "Oh, I mean before, in 1944."

Suddenly, his face closed. Now, it seemed, he had nothing to say. "No," he said curtly, and left. But his behavior made us uneasy and reluctant to explore.

We headed out and walked to Sip utca 12, the local Jewish community center where Eva and Alice had helped other Jews. We climbed to the top floor and looked down at the interior courtyard. Set in the middle of the 19th-century brick floor was a well-worn, large Star of David; I wished I could tell Eva it was still there.

The Jewish Forward — March 16, 2014

A GOOD NAME

I was named in memory of my paternal grandfather, Simon, a "kind, soft-spoken man," according to my mother. I learned this when I was 10-years-old, after my parents had divorced, and I was glad to know that although my mother detested my father, she had fond memories of her late father-in-law.

Like many first-generation Americans, my parents accepted some religious traditions and rejected others. They felt that the soul of a departed Jew could not rest until it was given new life when a baby was named for him or her. So they gave me a name that began with an "S," but did not give me a Hebrew name.

My immigrant grandparents also were subjective about which traditions they observed. What mattered most was to be "American," which meant modern and forward-thinking. After all, hadn't my maternal grandfather Aaron married my grandmother Esther (known as Etta), even though she and his mother had the same name? Most Ashkenazi Jews felt this was terrible and dangerous, because it might lead a man to have indecent thoughts about his mother, and—even worse—it might confuse the Angel of Death into taking the younger person's life by mistake.

But Aaron's mother, Esther Brondl, lived far away in Galicia. In America, you married for love. Aaron met Etta at a dance held on Manhattan's Lower East Side. He was captivated by her, but initially did not pursue her because of her name. The following year, he saw her again, and decided that he would no longer be controlled by *bubbemeister* superstitions. Esther Brondl died less than two years after my grandparents married. They named their next-born baby with a "B," for Brondl, fulfilling the tradition as best they could.

Aaron worked hard and made plenty of money. He provided well for his family, paid for his widowed father and siblings to come to America, and helped his brothers-in-law establish their businesses. But no babies would ever be named in Aaron's memory because, after twenty-seven years of marriage, Etta left him near the end of the Great Depression. Their grown children said that he brought it on, himself. Horrible quarrels and bad financial decisions had made Etta physically ill. The fights were so intense that she was forced to leave him. Afterwards, the children sided with their mother, and they, too, broke with Aaron.

I regret that I barely knew Aaron, but I grew up in Etta's home, where asking about him was asking for trouble. My own parents' divorce was a lot for me to handle, and Etta was a good and loving grandparent, my only source of constant, unconditional love. She died shortly before I was married, and by then, we all assumed that Aaron was dead, also.

Recently, I learned that Aaron had outlived Etta, and died when I was pregnant with my first-born son. My husband and I named him "Edward," in memory of Etta, and "Andrew" simply because we liked the name. We never considered naming a child after Aaron.

Since then, I've listened to Etta's three daughters, and reconsidered their versions of why their parents' marriage failed. Surely, Aaron mismanaged their money, and "practically threw us out of the building," recalled their youngest daughter. But wasn't Etta wrong to encourage their children to lose touch with him later on? I knew that he attended synagogue, observed the holidays, and supported Jewish causes. To have his name memorialized would have mattered to Aaron. Maybe he was not the kind of man to reminisce in regret but I imagine there were times during his long, last years alone, when he might have wondered if the curse that killed his mother after he married Etta had eventually poisoned their marriage, too. Was the price he paid for deceiving her greater than he should have borne?

I did not, consciously, choose an "A" for my son's middle name, but when I ponder the arc of my grandfather's life—how he rose from poverty to prosperity, was an acceptable if not extraordinary husband and father until he tumbled to the depths of rage and despair through bad decisions brought on by frightening and unforeseen economic times—I believe that Aaron deserved to have a descendant named for him, in spite of all that he did wrong.

"Everything that happens, happens as it should. You will find this is true, if you watch narrowly," wrote Marcus Aurelius in "Meditations" more than 1800 years ago. Sometimes, we do things but we don't know why. So tell me, was choosing "Andrew" a coincidence, or was it meant to be?

The Jewish Week of New York — February 17, 2006

BEARING WITNESS IN UKRAINE

"**B**ut you won't see anything," my aunt said, when I told her I was going to Ukraine to visit our family's ancestral towns. "It's all gone, every bit." Then she smiled and added whimsically: "Who knows – maybe you'll find modern shopping malls!"

Born in New York City in 1920, my aunt was the youngest daughter of immigrants who came from towns in western Galicia (now Ukraine) at the turn of the last century. She has always supported my work and my ambitions, and I'm sure that she didn't mean to disparage my plans. But she didn't understand that I almost didn't care if I found "nothing," (which I strongly doubted) or even shopping malls. For hundreds of years, a vibrant Jewish way of life had endured in Galicia and Bukovina. Now, I needed to find whatever remained of synagogues, cemeteries and Jewish neighborhoods, or stand before what was there now. What mattered was to show up, bear witness and remember.

In Lvov (formerly Lemberg), Zbarazh, Skalat and Chernivitsi (formerly Czernowitz), I would walk the streets of what had been the Jewish parts of town, and imagine shopkeepers in their stores, mothers tending children, boys studying in cheders, and people chatting in the streets. And maybe, if I was lucky (or unlucky, depending on your viewpoint), I would find traces from that long ago time.

I headed east toward my own personal heart of darkness. In Lvov, I touched notches in doorways where *mezuzot* had been affixed, and pressed my hands against stone walls where, from the 15th to 19th centuries, iron gates had slammed shut every night to close off the Jewish ghetto. Even so, drunken rowdies broke in periodically and besieged the little neighborhood with fierce pogroms. At the rubble-strewn site of what had been the Golden Rose Synagogue, erected in 1537, is a plaque describing its destruction by the Nazis in August 1941. Scrawled in black over the inscription was a swastika, attesting to undying anti-Semitism, even today.*

Memorial signs implore us to remember. At the edge of Lvov, all that remains of the notorious Janowska Concentration Camp is a series of wind-swept hillsides. Beneath them are the ashes of more than 200,000 Jews, buried in mass graves. "Passerby, stop. Bow your head!" a sign demands. "Here, the ground is suffering!" According to survivors' testimonies, bodies of the dead were exhumed before war's end so every last piece of value could be extracted from the decaying corpses which were then burned to nothingness and buried again. "Let the innocent undone victims be remembered forever! Eternal damnation on the executors!"

I stared at railroad tracks that surely had strained under the gruesome weight of relentlessly moving cattle cars, and train stations such as Kleparov, which—according to a plaque in the station waiting room—"served as passage for all Galician Jews on their way to death. About 500,000 Jews passed here in trains from March 1942 till the beginning of 1943."

In Zbarazh and Chernivitsi, I peeked into the windows of synagogues which had been torched, seized and eventually converted into factories, storehouses and movie theaters. In Skalat, the Jewish cemetery had been totally obliterated, and was now a soccer field. Where could I say *Kaddish*? Everywhere.

As my eyes scanned the site of the wartime "transit area" for Lvov's Jews, I thought of a friend of mine, in America, who had recounted the story of her deliverance from here. She was barely three-years-old in 1941 when her newly widowed mother hurled her over a barbed wire fence, and then climbed over, too, because she had figured out that this place was the gateway to their deaths. In the sixty-six year old haze of childhood memories, my friend recalls being wrapped in a thick shearling coat to cushion her fall, and that the hem of her mother's coat ripped on a wire, and diamonds fell to the ground. Her mother scooped them up, grabbed her daughter and ran. For the next four years, she worked as a cook (with false identity papers) for unsuspecting German soldiers, and paid farmers and nuns to care for my friend. Only later would she be called a "hidden child."

Usually, the memorial signs I saw were written in English, as well as Ukrainian. At first, I was just thankful that I could read the words, but then I realized there was a bigger message here: we are writing this in English not for the local people but for you – Americans especially, and others of the widespread English-language world. Read this, the memorials demand, and remember.

One day in the not-too-distant future the very last Holocaust survivor will have died, and it will be our responsibility as witnesses to tell the stories of their lives, their deaths, and of their homelands, again and again.

I saw plenty. And I will remember everything.

The Jewish Week of New York — April 20, 2007

* Author's note: In July 2008, according to the Jewish Telegraphic Agency, "a group of Jewish tourists from France found the vandalized plaque with a hangman's noose and a Star of David painted on it."

IN THE KILLING FIELDS OF SKALAT

"We can't go there," said my Ukrainian guide, as we sat in his van by an open field. It was late fall in Ukraine, and the air was piercingly raw. "The ground is too muddy to drive across."

"Can't we walk?" I asked.

"No, I'm sorry. We would sink if we tried."

We were on the outskirts of Skalat, one of my ancestral towns. In the distance, amid clumps of gray snow and the stubbled remains of harvested crops, was the memorial and site of the "Wailing Graves" where more than 750 Jews were murdered in April, 1943.

The butchery went on all day. That night, a gasping 17-year-old girl named Rebeka was pulled from the blood-soaked abyss by Lucy Baras, another survivor from Skalat.* In later years, Rebeka would recall that three square-shaped pits had been dug weeks before by Jews who thought the trenches were for storing phosphates for spring planting, or gasoline for the war effort. Instead, on a sunny day shortly before Passover, most of the last Jews of Skalat had been force-marched or carted to the edges of the pits and shot, one by one, by Nazi soldiers. At first, the victims were gunned down in groups of four, then groups of ten. Pistols were replaced by machine guns to speed up the process, and children were hurled into the pits alive.

Finally, dirt was shoveled over the "heaving" graves by other Jews, who then were shot, too.

Stories about the shootings of 1.5 million Jews in Ukraine between 1941—1944 had been suppressed by the Soviets for decades. But in 2002, nagging curiosity about his French grandfather's incarceration in Rawa-Ruska, a German concentration camp in western Ukraine, compelled Catholic priest Patrick Desbois to search for and identify what have become, so far, 850 mass grave sites. Within two years, he and a small crew of photographers and interpreters had embarked on their mission with funding from organizations including Yad Vashem, the US Holocaust Memorial Museum, and Yahad in Unum (which mean "together" in Hebrew and Latin), which Desbois established to search for the graves. So far, almost 1000 aged Ukrainian witnesses have given testimony to atrocities they've remembered since childhood.

"You're looking to know about the shootings of the Jews?" asked an old woman. "I was here." She and her neighbors had never spoken out before, even though their houses were barely a stone's throw from once-open pits.

Desbois has been recounting his experiences throughout the United States and Europe, and in his recent book, <u>The Holocaust By Bullets</u>. I, personally, sensed the power of his dedication when I met and heard him speak at the Museum of Jewish Heritage in Manhattan. In August, he will be the keynote speaker at the International Conference on Jewish Genealogy in Philadelphia.

"These people want absolutely to speak before they die," says Debois. "They want to say the truth."

In town after town, he asked them simple, straightforward questions: "Do you remember when the Germans came here?" "Did you see this for yourself?" "How many shootings did you see?" "Where are the corpses?" "Who killed them?" "Where are the graves?"

Sometimes, the old Ukrainians said, they had watched furtively from their family's attic windows as neighbors and childhood friends were hauled away at gunpoint and shot in nearby fields. Other times, the Nazis "requisitioned" Ukrainian children to climb trees and toss down human body parts blown up with explosives, or serve food to the shooters at meal tables set beside open graves. In return, the soldiers gave them sweets and candies while they were shooting. Images of bare-footed "requisitioned" girls stomping on bodies in the pits were almost beyond belief or understanding. Like winemakers crushing grapes in an upside-down, Bizarro world (which it was), they pushed down corpses with their feet so more bodies could be piled on top. Everyone didn't die immediately, and "the ground moved for days."

At first, what provoked Desbois were the same kinds of questions that prod people who have grown up wondering about suppressed stories in their families' histories. "Rawa-Ruska echoed like a painful family mystery," he explains. I know that kind of feeling well. It's when our personal stories touch on historical events that we zero in to uncover the details. As Jews we connect with every Holocaust story because every Jew lost was part of our family. At times, we can almost hear their words.

"Farewell life!" cried a doomed Jewish boy, making a faint gesture of goodbye to Anna, his Ukrainian schoolmate.

Moments later, he was shot to death. Sixty-one years after, Anna tearfully described that horrific day; it was the first time anyone had ever asked her about it.

In spring, 1944, after the Soviets drove the Germans out of Skalat, several dozen survivors emerged from nearby forests or other hiding places, and observed Passover on April 7th. That July, they circled the mass graves three times and asked forgiveness for surviving when so many had perished. Those with the gut-wrenching strength to relive their ordeals wrote down everything they remembered in memoirs and a *Yizkor* book.

The Jewish Week of New York — October 16, 2009

* Author's Note: In 1995, Lucy Rothstein Baras (b Lusia 1913 Skalat, d 2002 Sheboygan WIS) donated her 60,000-word memoir, <u>Twentieth-Century Cavemen</u>, to the University of Wisconsin-Milwaukee, where it is kept in the Archives. Her book describes her experiences living in Skalat, a largely Jewish village in Ukraine, and focuses mainly on the time of the Red Army invasion in 1939, followed by years of brutal conditions of life and death under the Germans and Ukrainians, until the end of the war.

HUNTING A DEAD NAZI

S.S. Sturmbannfuhrer Hermann Mueller was the Gestapo chief who commanded the deportations and exterminations of Galician Jews in the Tarnopol region from 1941 to 1943. His name is cursed like Amalek by Holocaust survivors, and my journey into Jewish genealogy prompted me to learn more about him. Most important, I wanted to know, what had happened to this butcher known as *"blutiger Judenfeind"* (bloody enemy of the Jews) who orchestrated the deaths of thousands in my ancestral towns.

I came across Mueller's name in "The Encyclopedia Judaica" the first time I looked up my grandfather's birthplace, Zbarazh, a town not far from Tarnopol, and read that the roundups, mass slaughters and deportations were all directed by him. Subsequently, I pursued my investigations in history books and *Yizkor* books, and online at websites including *www.ushmm.org* and *www. deathcamps.org*. I also met with Carl Modig, an archivist (now retired) at the United States Holocaust Memorial Museum in Washington, and found the birth date of the fiend I had begun to call "my Nazi," and which narrowed down my search immeasurably. Modig also provided rich biographical material about Mueller's military service and fanatical loyalty to the Nazi party.

At the U.S. National Archives and Records Administration in College Park, MD, I uncovered additional information in the vast collection of World War II papers that are part of the Berlin Documents File. The files also reinforced my belief in the essential need to save historical records as proof of their authenticity.

Born in Essen, Germany in 1909, Mueller was an uninspired school dropout when he joined the up-and-coming National Socialist German Workers' Party (Nazi party) in 1927. In subsequent years, he was jailed repeatedly for "agitations" and participation in violent riots. His 1938 SS personnel file describes him as "Catholic," "conscientious," "ambitious," "strongly bold," "articulate" and a "good organizer" and "enforcer." His "Nordic" appearance is borne out by his pale, austere face in a photograph. With his officer's cap tipped jauntily to one side, Mueller stares hard at the camera. It is a face that could easily haunt your dreams.

At war's end, Mueller evaded capture, changed his name and slipped into the British zone in Berlin. Hiding in plain sight in the northwestern city of Espelkamp, he married his third wife who bore him a son, and sold food in a small market operated under her name. Altogether, Mueller enjoyed fifteen years of freedom until he was arrested in 1961. Five years later, he and other former Nazi henchmen were tried in Stuttgart for the murders of Jews in the Tarnopol area.

Mueller's name is on almost every page of the lengthy trial report. My knowledge of German is scant, but with the help of a German-speaking member of my synagogue, I understood most of the material. We read about Dr. Jakob Wolf Gilson, who had survived imprisonment in a slave labor camp under Mueller's control, and testified that Mueller "would shoot children, women, any Jew he would chance upon, like one might shoot rabbits." His statement reminded me of another survivor's story about how Mueller ordered his soldiers to herd Jews awaiting transport into impossibly crowded areas and shoot anyone who couldn't sit down.

On the 38th day of the proceedings, Mueller broke down in tears, shocking everyone in the courtroom, and admitted (at least) some of his guilt. Facing Gilson, whose parents had perished in the Belzec gas chambers, Mueller begged for forgiveness. "It was everything terrible, what we did," he wept. Found guilty, he was sentenced to life imprisonment.

But few convicted Nazis served their entire sentences; had Mueller? Or did he die peacefully at home, in the warm embrace of his family? The answer required a lot of digging, but when I finally learned that he had died in prison, 22 years after being sentenced, I felt a grim satisfaction.

There is world history, and there is personal history. Recently, I visited the Zbarazh section in Beth David Cemetery in Queens, to say *Kaddish* before a monument for the 5,122 Jews murdered in my grandfather's town, including his first cousins. The prosecutors in Stuttgart had called them "Jews of Zbarazh," but were they? As Jews, they had always been outsiders, and although they had lived there since the 15th century, were they ever really from Zbarazh?

The Jewish Week of New York — November 19, 2010

SHINING STARS

First night of Hanukkah

WEARING MY JEWISH STAR

I haven't worn my Star of David since I was in high school years ago. Now, I've started wearing it again.

I've always preferred to be private about my religion. When I was a child, my family name didn't "sound" Jewish, and people always said I didn't "look it." That was fine with me; what I was, was nobody's business. Besides, virtually everyone in our neighborhood was Jewish; Gentiles were "different," not us. Things changed, however, when I was fourteen, and my family and I moved to a religiously mixed community. In my new high school, many teenage girls wore gold religious crosses, which bounced and glittered against their pastel-colored sweater sets.

"I want a Jewish star," I told my parents. For the first time in my life, I felt like an outsider. Wearing a star would be my quiet way of saying I was Jewish. Now I realize not only did I need to identify my religion to my classmates, I also needed to identify myself to me.

Other Jewish friends recount similar stories of adolescent interest in religious trappings. Interconnected with the desire to establish our independence from our families was the need to assert our identities, as well as the deep-rooted realization that no matter what we did or said, the rest of the world would always see us as Jews.

I wore my star throughout high school, and put it away when I entered college. By then, I was more secure in my self-concept, and didn't need a visible symbol to tell people who I was. For a long time, my star remained inside my jewelry box, next to other cherished pieces I don't wear anymore but would never throw away.

Today, I've taken out my star again, but unlike those people who always wear religious jewelry, I remain conflicted and ambivalent. Wearing a Jewish star in synagogue is one thing; wearing it to a Christmas party or job interview is something else. ("Tuck it inside," says a small voice in my head, "and you won't make trouble for yourself.")

Now, sometimes I wear my star for my original reason—to respond to all the crosses I see. This year, crosses have become a major fashion statement. Designers such as Donna Karan string them on jet black rosary-like chains, and an upscale department store catalog proclaims that "the new accessory of merit is the cross."

A Christian friend tells me she's offended by this crass commercialization because it debases her serious religious feelings. She also wonders—"Do Jews buy this jewelry? How do they feel about wearing a cross?" I hope they'd hate it. People who put on glitzy oversized crosses and think they're just being "fashionable" are wrong. I'm angry with retailers and fashion designers who think it's okay to take anything—no matter how sacred—and turn it into something money-making and tasteless.

My filigreed Star of David hangs from a fine gold chain. Sometimes I wear it so people can see it; other times I wear it for the comfort it gives me. I tuck it inside my blouse and—like amulets worn since ancient times—it's my little secret, sending out invisible rays of protection.

"When do you feel particularly Jewish?" asks my rabbi, encouraging my study group to reflect on living in a predominantly Christian society.

"When I'm with a group of people and everyone's Jewish," I realize. "And when I'm with a group and no one's Jewish but me. And . . . when I'm wearing my Jewish star."

Wearing it in public, of course, can be risky. You wear your star on a public bus and somebody shoves you; is that why? . . . or you argue with a dishonest shopkeeper, see him look at your star and know he's probably thinking. Humph! She's Jewish, so no wonder she's haggling and complaining about the price!

Not long ago, as I packed for a two-week trip to Europe, I debated if I should take my star. Should I be wearing it in airports? In foreign countries, where who knew who might be looking at me? Okay, I thought, I'll wear it inside my clothing, private and safe, and just for me. But feelings of comfort couldn't compete against deeper gut-level fears of being identified, and putting myself at unnecessary risk.

This fear of being "found out" to be a Jew is, unfortunately, very old and very real. Even if you don't announce your "Jewishness," you're always at risk for being "found out." I thought about Islamic terrorists singling out Jewish hostages on captured airplanes, and Jews I know who own two passports—one filled with customs stamps from Israel, and the other for the rest of the world. Paradoxically, at the same time talismans are supposed to be protecting us, they also can expose us to potential harm.

That doesn't stop me from wearing my star, although I do pick and choose when and where this happens. For the past few years, I've been volunteering at an after-school tutoring center for homeless children. Most of the children are Black. None are Jews. According to a recent survey by the Anti-Defamation League of B'nai B'rith, more than a third of all American Blacks are strongly anti-Semitic. The less educated, the more prejudiced they are likely to be. With so many tensions existing between Blacks and Jews today, it's no longer enough for me to be "just" a volunteer. Some of the families were evicted from houses owned by Jewish landlords, but how many Jews do these kids actually meet? They already know I care about them. Now I also want them to know that I'm Jewish. Wearing my Star of David is my silent way of telling them.

When I was growing up, my parents were divorced, and that made me "different" enough. All I wanted was to blend in. But the homeless kids I tutor can't do this. In some ways, their Black skin is their "star;" it's an undeniable thing that they can't remove.

But—I don't see their color anymore. They're not Black kids. They're just kids to me. Our colors "reappear" when we go outside the building. Walking down the street, we are a distinctive group. Passersby barely notice me, but the children are "those Black kids from the welfare hotel."

Considering how bleak and sad their lives have been, most of the children are remarkably resilient, Their young eyes are still soft-looking and gentle, and are not hardened with anger at the system which lets them down. There is still time for me to make a difference in their lives.

I have been wearing my star to the tutoring center every week; for quite a while, no one said anything about it. Then, a little girl was interested. She touched it gently and asked me what it was.

"It's something Catholics wear," said her big brother right away.

"No way," said his friend, shaking his head. "It's a Jewish star, right?"

I nodded and smiled.

"Are you Jewish?" they asked.

"Yes," I replied.

And that was it. No great conversation; just an acknowledgment. So even if we never talk more about it, I hope they will remember me, and remember my star. Their mothers notice it, when they drop by the center. We chat for a while and they glance at my star. And although nothing is said, something has been said after all.

Lilith — Summer 1994

STAR SIGHTINGS

"Common sense is all you need, Just use good judgment. Tourists aren't really a target in Israel," said a sweet-voiced young woman when I telephoned the Israeli Tourist Office in Manhattan. My husband and I were going to Jerusalem soon, and I had shared my trepidation and concern about our safety.

"Just don't do anything provocative."

"Provocative?"

"Like wearing a Star of David in the Arab quarter."

"Oh."

Actually, I had intended to wear my Star all the time. It's not some-thing I do everyday in New York, but, after all, I was going to Israel. If a Jew can't wear her Star of David there... where can she?

"And another thing," the woman continued. "Wear a camera around your neck; that way, you won't look like an Israeli."

OK, so ... I'd probably be safe in Israel, as long as I didn't look like a Jew or a citizen. Tricky stuff for someone like me. I always feel as if I'm going home when I visit Israel, even though I have no family or friends there.* I love walking the streets of Tel Aviv in silent, soul-satisfying amazement that virtually everyone around me is Jewish. That's why being "labeled" a Jew in Israel was not something I had worried about. How could this precious talisman, which gives me comfort and probably a naive sense of protection, also expose me to potential harm?

Probably, there's no safe time to visit Israel, but these days, there are no safe places anywhere. Random violence is much too prevalent. Whenever I travel, I worry about the usual things—lost luggage, food poisoning, petty thieves and pickpockets. But going to Israel also meant worrying about the PLO and religious extremists. Maybe tourists weren't "targets," but what about Jewish tourists? Is it courage, or foolhardiness, to reveal you're a Jew in risky situations?

I had planned to wear my Jewish Star everywhere in Israel... in airports, on planes, in hotels, museums, restaurants, on streets in the Old City... but I began to have second thoughts soon after I left my house. Even in New York, wearing a star in public can be risky. You wear it on the subway and somebody shoves you; is that why? You argue with an unscrupulous shopkeeper and see him glance at your star. He's probably thinking, so that's why she's haggling and complaining about the price!

Revealing my star and concealing it became a motif of my entire trip. It was tucked inside my collar at JFK airport, and pulled out after I boarded my EL AL plane. Inside when I rode in a *sherut* to my hotel in Jerusalem, and outside after I checked in. Inside at the Dome of the Rock, outside at Yad Vashem. Inside when I shopped in the Armenian Quarter, outside (and fingered lovingly) as I recited prayers at the Western Wall.

In the Jewish Quarter of the Old City, an elderly man stared at my Jewish Star and accosted me. "Jesus, Jesus," he whispered. Then he squeezed my arm gently, and shuffled away. At the Israel Museum, I approached a group of German tourists viewing an exhibit on the Jewish cycle of life. *"Schnippen, schnippen!"* said their tour leader playfully, moving his fingers like scissors and pointing to items in a showcase. Members of the group snickered and a few laughed heartily. Eyes darted around self-consciously; someone noticed my Star and looked away. After they vacated the room, I walked over to the showcase and saw that it contained ceremonial objects for circumcisions.

Unlike people who always wear religious jewelry, I'm ambivalent about it. Wearing a Star in my synagogue is one thing; wearing it to a job interview is something else. ("Tuck it inside," says a small voice inside my head. "And you won't make trouble for yourself.") The last time I wore my Star of David continually was when I was in high school. My family and I had moved from a neighborhood in Queens where, it seemed, everyone was Jewish, to a mixed community on Long Island where Jews were in the minority. I needed a Star, if only to offset the shiny gold crosses dangling from the necks of all those Catholic girls. Not only did I need to identify myself to my classmates, but I needed to identify myself to myself.

I've never worn any other symbols of Judaism, not a *Chai*, a *hamsa* or anything else. A Star of David is very direct. No question about it, the wearer is a Jew. And I think that's one of the things I like about it. When it's "out," I'm a Jew. Tucked inside, my religion is my business, and you don't know what it is... unless I choose to tell you.

The Jewish Week of New York — July 2, 1999

* Author's Note: This piece was published barely one month before I first located and contacted Eva, and returned to Israel in December 1999. Soon after that, I found other cousins, too. Similar words appear in "Wearing My Jewish Star" too.

RESTORING A PRE-HOLOCAUST TORAH, AND A FAMILY

Days before the 2016 Presidential election in America, my husband Ken and I flew from New York to Sydney, Australia. Our decision to vote by absentee ballot and travel almost 10,000 miles from home was to witness the installation of my late great-uncle Jacob's restored pre-Holocaust Torah in a modern Orthodox synagogue in a suburb of Sydney.

At the time, however, we didn't realize that our understanding of the Torah's history would not be the same as that of the newly discovered cousins who had contacted us, and whom we would meet, soon, in Sydney. Everything I knew about the Torah had been told to me by my elderly second cousin, Eva, granddaughter of Jacob and, in many ways, the keeper of the stories of our family's past.

Six months earlier, my memoir, <u>Because of Eva: A Jewish Genealogical Journey</u>, had been published by a prestigious university press. After that, it had been read, I learned, by relatives I didn't know—including one of Jacob's grandsons, Danny.

The Torah was already on the *bimah* at Central Synagogue in Bondi Junction when Ken and I entered the sanctuary. He and other male relatives were invited to "ink in" the final letters, which they did proudly. When the ink dried, the Torah was rolled up, wrapped in its mantle, and topped with a majestic silver crown. Singing and dancing men crowded around it joyously, lifted it up, and carried it to its new home in the Ark.

While the story of Jacob's Torah is heart-warming and uplifting, it is not simple. I heard it first, in 2002, from Eva, who was Jacob's oldest grandchild. She and I were sitting in the living room of her Tel Aviv home, barely half a mile from the beaches by the Mediterranean Sea, but more than 1300 miles away from her birthplace in Budapest, and decades away in time.

"Before the war," she began. We both knew which war—the war in Europe, the war in which millions of Jews were murdered, including members of our own family. Eva continued: "My mother's father, Jacob, was the president of the Kazinczy synagogue in Budapest, and in the 1930s he had donated a sefer Torah to it. Jacob had come to Budapest around 1895, after leaving his home town of Zbarazh in Galicia. He had married Chava Beulah already, and later on, I would be named for her."

Eva was in her 80s and she was sharing many stories with me about her life before, during, and after World War II. She was well-educated, bright, honest and straightforward, and until her death in 2010, she told her stories without embellishment or exaggeration.

As we sat together in two comfortable armchairs, I glanced at a tall bookcase crammed with books written in English, Hebrew, Hungarian, German and French, and thought about how much Eva always loved to read. Books had been her lifeline and escape many times, from the terrors surrounding her long ago. In late fall, 1944, as Allied bombs fell on Budapest, she had crouched in a corner of her quaking apartment and read Thomas Mann's The Magic Mountain. Food and water were terribly scarce, but books were always there. Now, she placed a bowl of Clementines and dried dates on a nearby coffee table and offered them to me. I smiled, shook my head no, and she continued to describe that horrifying time.

In March, 1944, shortly before the Germans invaded Budapest and subsequently shut down all Jewish houses of worship, prescient members of Jacob's synagogue removed all the Torahs from the Ark, hid and buried them... somewhere. Over the next nine months, bombings, lootings, shootings and raging fires brought massive destruction and many deaths. By fall, "there was no order, only madness and chaos," said Eva. When the Soviets drove out the Nazis early in 1945, "we accepted the fact that the Torah was lost."

By then, Jacob, his second wife Klara, their youngest daughter, Suzi (18-years-old) and, possibly, one or two older children had emerged from hiding and were living in a small apartment. Twenty-four-year old Eva was there one day when a Hungarian Nazi soldier walked in, with a rucksack on his back. She recalled how fearful the family was, especially when the soldier asked, specifically, for Jacob.

"'Yes?' my grandfather whispered, knowing a Jew's life was very cheap in those days," Eva told me.

The soldier insisted on speaking privately to Jacob, and then confessed that he, too, was a Jew and his uniform was a disguise. Next, he opened his sack, pulled out the sefer Torah, and presented it to Jacob, saying, "I found it and kept it for you."

"Jacob didn't live much longer," said Eva, "But at least he could hold his Torah. Later on, it was brought to Israel."

The day after Eva told me this story, I went to the "Big Synagogue" in Ramat Gan and saw the sefer Torah in a room where it was stored with other Torahs no longer kosher because of small imperfections and damages. Neither I nor my Israeli cousin, Avi, who accompanied me, could find any errors; nor could the congregant who assisted us. But he also reminded us that just one non-kosher letter in a Torah scroll can make the entire scroll non-kosher. Even so, we were pleased. It's not perfect, we thought, but it was rescued and saved, and it is here, in Israel.

However, we did notice that one of the four wooden Torah handles was different from the others. While they were light in color, smooth and plain, this handle was definitely older, made of darker wood, with deeply etched, decorative lines. Encircling the roller plate was a silver band engraved with the letter, "M."

Why an "M?" I wondered. "Why not a "J" ... for Jacob? Or a "Y," for Yacov?"

"Maybe the 'M' is for Moshe, Jacob's father and my great-grandfather," Avi suggested. "Since he and the whole family were originally from Zbarazh, it's likely that's where the Torah really came from." That made sense. Later on, after we researched immigration records and other historical documents, Avi and I also were also pretty sure that in 1923, when Moshe left Zbarazh to immigrate to New York with his son, my grandfather Aaron, they stopped in Budapest on their way to America. Since Jacob was Moshe's eldest and most religious son, it's likely that Moshe would have entrusted his Torah to him.

Eventually, I wrote about all this in <u>Because of Eva</u>, which was published in spring, 2016. In it, I explained why and how mysteries in my family prodded me to delve into World War II and Holocaust history. My entire search for family had been motivated by curiosity and my need to repair branches on my family tree that had been broken by war, immigration, my grandparents' marital separation and my parents' divorce. I also raised questions about the accuracy of old family stories that we can no longer prove or disprove.

A few months later, Danny, a second cousin I never knew, read my memoir in Sydney, Australia, and learned the location of his grandfather Jacob's Torah. Danny also told his elderly mother, Suzi, about it. She was the only one of Jacob's children who was still alive. Suzi said that in 1935, Jacob's children gave him the sefer Torah as a birthday gift in Budapest, when she was about nine years old. She assumed that it was new, but was it? Or was it Moshe's "old" Torah that his grandchildren had repaired and made kosher for Jacob?

Sometimes, writers receive unexpected pay-offs when their words spur readers into action. Forthwith, Danny flew from Sydney to Israel and arranged for the Torah to be restored. After that, it was brought to Central Synagogue, for a ceremony called a *"Hachnasat"*—the installation of a Torah scroll.

One of the trickiest parts about recording family histories is the difficulty (and sometimes, the impossibility) of confirming what really happened in the past. As most of us know, what one person remembers to be true is not, necessarily, another person's recollection. We like to think we remember everything correctly; after all, we were there, we should know. But sometimes, what we remember is only a small part of a much larger picture, what we have been told by others, or what we wish had happened. We like to think our memories are crystal clear... but they aren't. Maybe the event we recall didn't really happen that way.

Probably, when Eva told me about the Torah, she knew even more than she said. I didn't ask, "Was it new?" "What was its history?" "Where did it come from?" Now, I wish I had. But Eva's stories about the war years came fast; when she finished one, she quickly moved on to another. It was like opening windows on a long-shuttered room.... So I didn't ask Eva anything else about the Torah, because I thought, this is its history.

The *Hachnasat* of Jacob's (or his father Moshe's?) Torah was celebrated in the Central Synagogue in Bondi Junction on Suzi's 90th birthday in November, 2016. "Nothing is more treasured than a Torah scroll, which is the heart of every synagogue," said Rabbi Levi Wolf. "We celebrate the homecoming of a pre-Holocaust Torah that escaped, survived, and is reborn."

The Torah was on the *bimah* when Ken and I saw it, but now all the handles had been replaced by freshly polished ones and encased in silver. The "M" was gone.

As I watched the Torah being carried from the *bimah* to the Ark, I thought—We will never know for sure this Torah's beginnings, but that's okay, for this is not just a story about the past, it's also a story of who we are now.

Here is the Torah, brought back to full life in a synagogue, and such a *mitzvah* is a very good thing.

BEARING WITNESS IN FLORENCE

On a drizzly Sunday morning in November, 1993, my husband, Ken, and I walked along Via Farini in Florence, heading toward the synagogue. It was our third trip to Italy, fulfilling my wish to celebrate my (fast-approaching) 50th birthday in my favorite foreign country. Some days, we had raced around, attempting to visit every site on a preconceived, well-thought-out list of "must sees." But we had no grand plans that day, except to see the ornate Moorish interior of the 19th century temple, and perhaps buy some mementos in the gift shop.

Most travelers have experienced the excitement of intending to do this... but doing that instead. You get off a train at the wrong stop, walk the opposite way down a street, or turn a corner and come upon an unexpected but glorious garden, or a tiny restaurant with out-of-this-world food, or a man who reminds you of a long-forgotten friend. Something happens. You see someone or do something that wasn't supposed to happen. And yet it did.

On the day after *Shabbat*, we had expected to find the synagogue deserted, but hundreds of people were streaming into the courtyard and the building. This was no holiday crowd, spirited and joyous. Few spoke; they walked steadily, somberly, and deliberately—teenagers hunched together, parents carrying small children, and old people leaning on canes or on one another. We followed, swept along as much by the steady flow of people as by our own curiosity. Guards stopped us at the iron gate; what did we want? We'd been questioned before, at Jewish houses of worship; incidents of violence were always anticipated. We're Jews from New York, we explained in broken Italian, as I opened my handbag for their inspection. All right, they nodded, and let us by.

We sat in the last row of the sanctuary, on either side of the center aisle separating men and women. Soon, all the seats were filled, and more people stood in clumps behind us or in the galleries upstairs. Green pamphlets rested on the wooden armrests. We couldn't read Italian, but managed to decipher the words on the cover: "*Communita Ebraica Firenze 50th anniversario dell' inizion della deportazione degil ebrei da Firenze.*"

On November 6 and 7, 1943, during the German occupation of Italy, the Jews of Florence, who had lived in the community for 450 years, were rounded up and deported by the Nazis. Of the 248 Florentines seized, 23 had been small children.

Now, for over an hour, the rabbi and survivors addressed the silent congregation. Knowing Italian wasn't necessary because words such as Nazis, Auschwitz, Treblinka, Sobibor, *madre, padre, bambini, crematoria,* and *tutta la familia* were understood all too easily. Sometimes, the elderly speakers paused, fighting back tears and gathering strength to continue their tragic tales. How much longer would any of them be alive to remember and tell what had happened?

The events they described had taken place fifty years ago, only five days before I was born in New York

City. I'm not a big believer in fate or predestination, but I couldn't help wondering, what complicated and elaborate path in my own life had led me—fifty years later—to be at that synagogue on that specific day? The survivors and descendants of the victims had planned to attend the memorial service, but what was I doing there?

On those two November days during World War II, most of the Jews of Florence had been forcibly taken away from their homes forever. Many were killed, including all the *bambini*. I looked around the packed synagogue and trembled. If I had been born in Florence, I would not be alive to bear witness to what happened. Now, quite possibly, I was the only person in the synagogue who was (almost exactly) 50 years old. Those who spoke were at least ten or fifteen years older than I. No Florentine Jew my age was alive to bear witness, but I could bear witness to the witnesses.

The cantor sang *"Ani Ma'amin,"* a mournful prayer and the concluding hymn, and everyone rose and silently walked outside. Once again, Ken and I followed the crowd and huddled on steps overlooking the enclosed courtyard. Rain was falling, and anyone with an umbrella opened it. Everybody huddled so closely together, we were all protected by the overlapping umbrellas. But out in the open, under a rain-drenched sky, survivors, religious leaders and dignitaries stood firmly at attention beside a plaque listing all the names of the deportees. Soaked to the skin, no one moved, as an honor guard of musicians played a funereal taps.

I brought the green pamphlet home from my trip, and tucked it away in a now-forgotten spot. Apparently,

I put it away for safekeeping so well that now I don't remember where it is. What I do have, however, are two hand-embroidered cloths purchased at the gift shop the following day. Maybe I don't need a tangible record of that heart-wrenching memorial service, but the exquisite cloths enhance my *Shabbat* table. They remind me of the surviving Florentine Jews who, with intricate, lovely stitches of thread, are creating beauty out of misery, and weaving powerful stories impossible to forget.

The Jewish Week of New York — October 30, 1998

WHEN THE DANUBE REALLY DID "RUN RED"

When the Hotel Astoria in Budapest opened in 1914, it imparted an aura of old-world style and tradition. Even today, the hotel evokes elegance and decorum, until you think about its more recent past.

On March 14, 1944, "large groups of German officers" were gathered in the lobby in mid-afternoon, "moving about ... talking ... laughing," writes Zsuzsanna Ozsvath in her gripping memoir, <u>When the Danube Ran Red</u> (Syracuse University Press). As her father subsequently explained, his sister Lulu had checked out of the Astoria that morning, left her suitcase by the reception area, and met him at a café. A few hours later, they came back for the suitcase, and were terrified to see all the officers. What they didn't know was that the Nazi occupation of Budapest had begun, and the hotel had been commandeered as Gestapo headquarters. Not surprisingly, her father "had been frozen over, his heart beating in his throat."

"Even today, just thinking about that hotel makes me catch my breath," Ozsvath writes.

Me, too. I felt the same way when I approached the Astoria in 2006 because I knew that my cousins, Eva and Alice, had been summoned there by the Gestapo in June 1944, and spared only because Swedish authorities intervened at the last minute and granted them life-saving Swedish citizenship.

Ozsvath, a professor of literature and the history of ideas, and chair of Holocaust studies at University of Texas at Dallas, has recorded harrowing memories from her Jewish childhood more than sixty-five years ago. I was drawn to her story partly because I'm always interested in child's-eye views of the world, and also because many of young "Zsuzsi's" recollections are amazingly similar to those told to me by Eva, who had been a resistance fighter in Budapest.

The Oszvaths survived the first six months of the occupation mainly because of the selfless devotion of their former nursemaid, "Erzsi" (Erzebet) Fajo, who supplied them with food and clothing. They scraped by until October 1944, when the nefarious *Niylas* (Hungarian Nazis) seized control of the city.

Erzsi began moving 13-year-old Zsuzsi from one safe place to another. In late December, as the Russians advanced on the beleaguered capital, she brought Zsuzsi to a riverfront apartment where a smiling woman promised to safeguard her in exchange for a gold-and-sapphire bracelet.

The next morning, bombs and artillery explosions awakened Zsuzsi, who soon realized that the woman had fled before dawn, taking the jewelry and last bits of food with her. Hearing gunfire, Zsuzsi crawled to a window and peeked through broken panes to see "a bunch of children, men, and women standing on the bank of the Danube, on their chests the palm-sized yellow star. They were bound together by ropes. At least four or five *Niylas* aimed their guns at them, shooting them into the river, which flowed red like blood. Nobody screamed, nobody cried. ... Nothing ... but the splash of the bodies falling into the red foam."

Remembering Erzsi's warnings not to seek shelter in the basement lest inquisitive tenants determine that she was a Jew-in-hiding, Zsuzsi hid inside a closet. It took Erzsi three days to rescue her.

By war's end, virtually all of Zsuzsi's friends and most of her extended family had been shot into mass graves or killed at Auschwitz. In 1946, Zsuzsi's parents adopted Erzsi as their own, and eventually she was named Righteous Among the Nations at Yad Vashem.

Not all Holocaust survivors have sufficient strength to record their memories, but those who do consign us stories of immeasurable power. We listen, and we read, and if the stories are good and true, we incorporate them into our own views of the world. What I've learned from Eva and Zszusi has affected my life ever since.

Five years ago, my husband and I entered the lobby of the Astoria. We eyed the ornate lounge and café, and were chilled by how much we knew. It was easy to imagine black-booted brutes guzzling schnapps and devouring cream cakes while singing schmaltzy tunes. Long before I concluded that the "blue" Danube was a river of death, I always felt that the lively melodies of that famous waltz smacked too much of Teutonic cheer.

In April 2005, a memorial called "Shoes on the Danube Bank" was erected beside the river in Budapest. In remembrance of Jews murdered during the winter of 1944-'45, sixty cast-iron replicas of men's, women's and children's shoes are anchored along a stone promenade. Some shoes are placed neatly in pairs, others as if they were kicked off in haste. Wall plaques describe how the wearers were tied together in threes, the middle victim was shot and the bodies tumbled into the icy water. Zsuzsanna Ozsvath had witnessed the horrors, and recorded the stories for all of us.

The Jewish Week of New York — April 29, 2011

THE SOUL OF POLDEK PFEFFERBERG

On Jerusalem's Mt. Zion, a plaque on a Christian cemetery gate announces "Oskar Schindler's Grave" and is the only clue that you've come to the burial site of the extraordinary German industrialist, womanizer and "black-marketeering Nazi" memorialized in the book and film, *Schindler's List.* But no signs point the way inside until you come upon one tombstone heaped with stones. Some are tiny pebbles, others are palm-sized rocks spread over everything except Schindler's name, birth and death dates, a cross, and words that sum up so much: "The unforgettable rescuer of 1,200 persecuted Jews."

I came to Schindler's grave this winter, long after reading Thomas Keneally's 1983 book. What motivated me was his latest work, "Searching for Schindler," which tells touching and even amusing behind-the-scenes stories of author and subjects. Possibly, the book should be called "The Perseverance of Poldek Pfefferberg," for surely, this *SchindlerJuden* is the hero of this saga.

In 1947, Poldek told Schindler, "You protected us and stayed with us until five minutes after midnight, and I will try to tell your story." Over forty years, he collected documents, memorabilia, and photographs attesting to Schindler's triumphs, feats and finagling. If not for Poldek's steadfast and unwavering determination, there would have been no book, and no Academy Award-winning film.

"There'll be an Oscar for Oskar!" he predicted to Steven Spielberg.

Poldek could charm and intimidate anyone, especially low-level bureaucrats. In humorous and reverential words, Keneally describes their tense encounter with a Polish soldier threatening to detain them at an airport because they were taking too much cash out of the country. The lengthy confrontation ended abruptly when Poldek adroitly praised the soldier's handsome Slavic features and enticed him with vague promises of a part in the multi-million dollar film "on World War II Polish history" that would certainly follow the not-yet-written book.

I met Poldek Pfefferberg in 1995, when he spoke at a college in southern California. My husband accompanied me, and soon realized he had met Poldek in Los Angeles years before. Like Keneally, who had wandered into Poldek's air-conditioned Beverly Hills leather goods store in 1980 to escape the heat and maybe find a new briefcase, Ken was lured inside by a shoe display, and the smiling shop-owner who beckoned from the window. But Ken was a Jewish New York lawyer between appointments, not a Catholic Australian novelist who knew little about the Holocaust, and even less about "Jewish suffering" – excellent reasons, Poldek insisted, why Keneally was the ideal person to write the book.

Poldek's audience that day was young, primarily Christian, and spellbound by the former Polish Jewish officer who'd been caught in the Nazis' grip and rescued by ... a member of the Nazi party. But Schindler's motives for success were personal, not political, and he soon determined that adequately feeding, protecting, and caring for his workers would make them more productive and keep them alive. Poldek also talked about his love for America and the values which defined his adopted home. "Democracy doesn't mean you can do whatever you want," he said. "It means you don't do anything to others that you don't want done to you.... It's when people don't speak up that innocent victims suffer...."

Afterwards, he joined Ken and me for lunch in the college cafeteria, and that's when Ken brought up the topic of his shoes. On that long-ago day in Beverly Hills, Ken – who had a weakness for fine Italian footwear – had spotted some in Poldek's window, and entered the store. In less time than it takes to reel in an unsuspecting fish, Poldek had sold Ken a pair of mustard-yellow Italian leather loafers which were very comfortable, but hideously ugly.

"I guess I was a good salesman!" Poldek laughed.

But the Holocaust is not a topic you fool around with; stories are either true or false. These days, I've grown quite weary of frauds – literary as well as monetary. We don't need any more fake Holocaust memoirs which belittle the truth and strengthen deniers' claims; no misrepresentations of historical facts; and no tricky balance sheets or unbelievable financial deals (which seem unbelievable because they really are).

Until his death in 2001, Poldek continued to speak to students, religious and military groups, evoking painful memories with heartfelt honesty. "We still see cracks of inhumanity around the world and do very little," he lamented. But the scathing lessons of racism and fascism must be learned to counter fanatics who promulgate "ethnic cleansing." They would do well to know about resolute men like Oskar Schindler and Poldek Pfefferberg, and reject those who play with our emotions by hideously distorting the truth.

The Jewish Week of New York — April 17, 2009

STORIES
WE NEVER HEARD

If you're lucky, you were raised on stories—big ones such as how family members immigrated to America, and small ones such as your aunt's first job. It doesn't matter how exotic or transforming the stories are, because even a mundane situation can bring forth a great tale.

I grew up hearing many stories, but some topics—especially those regarding the breakdowns of my parents' and grandparents' marriages – were strictly off limits. Even so, I wondered about the reasons, since I was affected by the fallout. My need to make sense of those cataclysmic rifts has compelled me to find distant relatives, search genealogical web sites, and follow all leads to uncover the facts.

For children whose parents survived the Holocaust, life was tinged by much greater sadness. Whether or not information was imparted about the terrible, horrifying past, an unremitting sense of loss and gloom lingered in the shadows. But now, second-generation children are writing and speaking about the Holocaust, from their personal and unique vantage points.

When Erin Einhorn's Jewish mother was a baby in wartime Poland, her father left her in the care of a Christian woman who sheltered and protected her until war's end. "I was loved," Erin's mother would say. Her brief stories were always recited in the same way, in a certain order, with few details unless Erin pressed hard for more information. At times, she felt caught between the fascination of what she knew, and fear of what she didn't.

"Memory is not the same as truth," Erin reflects in her memoir, *The Pages in Between: A Holocaust Legacy of Two Families, One Home*. But all versions of a story always have "some glimmer of truth." From 2001–2002, Erin lived in Poland to learn more about her mother's years as a hidden child, and to investigate the mysteries surrounding ownership of her family's house near Krakow, which Erin's grandfather had entrusted to the Christian woman as a form of payment for his daughter's care.

Discovering old stories is a race against time, because after the death of the last relative who was "there," stories leave "the realm of memory" and become "secondhand." By 2001, the Christian woman was dead, but her 71-year-old son shared his memories with Erin. In gratitude, she attempted to set things right by trying to pass ownership of the house to him. "Maybe reconciliation was meant to skip a generation," she says, "to be left to those of us for whom the past was not so personal."

Writer, storyteller and performer Lisa Lipkin could never escape from the stories she had not heard in childhood. "The only stories I know tumbled out, accidentally," she recounts in her CD, *What Mother Never Told Me: Reminiscences of a Child of a Holocaust Survivor*. Whatever she heard was scant and hastily described, such as the time her mother recalled furtively plucking berries off a tree, when she was imprisoned in a labor camp. Brief memories like these, stirred up out of the blue, would become Lisa's peculiar inheritance instead of typical family heirlooms passed down by the previous generation.

While Lisa's friends dreamed about the future, she worried about her mother's dreadful past. But the paucity of tales had a inspirational effect on Lisa, whose book, <u>Bringing The Story Home: The Complete Guide to Storytelling for Parents</u>, encourages families to narrate their own life stories and suggests simple ways in which children as young as three can do this.

On my journey to make sense of my own peculiar inheritance, I went looking for my second cousin, Eva, only because she had known my grandfather in New York. Stories about him were all that I expected, until she began describing, first-hand, the gruesome details of Jewish life in Budapest under the Nazis in 1944. From Eva, I also learned about members of our extended family who had been killed in the Holocaust. Listening to her stories was like watching one of those scenes in a film when a moving train speeds around a narrow bend and suddenly you see wide-open spaces of astounding scenery.

Since then, what keeps me going, besides my own unflagging curiosity, is the belief that, eventually, one of my descendants – a grandchild, perhaps – will be as inquisitive as I have been, and pursue my investigations even further. And maybe, he or she will share our stories, too.

The Jewish Week of New York — November 18, 2008

Author's Note: Unlike most of my work, this is not an opinion or thought piece. It's more informative and is about the telling of stories. I was very impressed by the works of the two Jewish writers cited above, which reinforce the importance of storytelling. Now, I wonder, what else might I have learned, if I had met Eva years ago? But then I think old age was her "right time," because that's when she was ready to talk.

WAXING NOSTALGIC: THE NINTH DAY OF CHANUKAH

During Chanukah, everyone talks about the Maccabees' long-ago victory over the armies of Antiochus, and what we call the Miracle of the Oil. It's been said that when the Maccabees returned, at last, to clean and restore the Temple, they poked through the rubble, and found eight iron spears that were fashioned into receptacles for oil. When the Eternal Light was lit with only one day's worth of oil and burned for eight days, it was deemed a miracle.

For centuries, we have spun *dreidels* and sung about Chanukah. Even though most of us light candles instead of oil these days, we continue to honor that historic event. Which is why I'm here to talk about the ninth day of Chanukah—the day after the Festival of Lights—when it's time to get the wax off your Chanukah menorah.

When I was a kid, my family had a menorah. It was made of brass, and had a graceful shape with four sweeping arms on each side of the *shamash* candleholder. Even though it held nine candles—not seven—we called it a menorah, not a chanukiah. All year, it stood on a cabinet shelf in the foyer. Shortly before the first night of Chanukah, our menorah was placed on the dining room sideboard, alongside a box of 44 candles. They were swirly and short, with stringy white wicks, and were identical, except for their colors—blue, red, white, green, orange and yellow. Usually, we set the red one in the *shamash* holder, but this was by habit, not because of any particular rule.

Cleaning the menorah was a good job for an elementary school-aged child, and I toiled assiduously to remove every speck of the previous night's wax. The work was particularly challenging if the melted globs of wax had run down the arms of our menorah, and oozed on to the filigreed base. If I skipped a day, I always regretted it, especially if the lit candles had bent toward each other and burned more quickly than usual. Even today, I never put off the task.

An informal survey has revealed the popular methods of menorah maintenance: removing the wax every day (humdrum but quick); at the end of eight days (more challenging and time-consuming); annually, right before it's used again (would you put away a wine-and-food-stained holiday tablecloth?); and ... not at all. I cannot even discuss this category.

Metal menorahs are easiest to clean; ceramic ones can crack under heat or pressure. My dentist's wife cleans her menorah with a fine pointy tool used to pick teeth, and says it does an excellent job. So does a Water Pik set on "high." Screwdrivers get in all the grooves but they can leave scratches and marks, unlike hot hair dryers which can just singe your hand.

Probably, the oldest and truest way to remove wax from a menorah is with your fingernails, which scrape nicely but do not scratch. Show me a Jew with beautifully manicured nails during Chanukah, and I'll show you someone with a waxy menorah.

Usually, I just pour boiling water over my menorah. I make sure to do this outdoors, not over my kitchen sink, so the wax doesn't clog up the drain. My friend places her menorah in the freezer for a few hours and say peeling off the wax is a breeze when she takes it out. Another friend puts her menorah in a large pot of boiling water until the wax loosens and rises to the surface. Then she turns off the heat and picks off the hardened wax floating on top.

Maybe what we need are fulltime waxscrapers—like those who work at Buddhist temples. Day after day, streams of supplicants pass by the altars, lighting candles and making offerings. The sole job of the waxscraper is to keep the vast array of candlesticks free from drippings.

Or... we could simply use electric menorahs. Although you do have to dust them now and then.

The Jewish Week of New York — November 30, 2007

TO SAVE ONE LIFE...

I n a hotel room in Amsterdam, I awakened to the smell of something burning. I wasn't alarmed, however, because I sensed quickly that the pungent odor was more annoying than dangerous, and that the hotel wasn't on fire.

The smell was worse when I opened a window. The overcast sky was dense, like a thick wall of soiled cotton. Coughing and sneezing, my husband and I showered and dressed, and ate a quick breakfast in our room. Then we went down to the lobby.

"What is that smell?" we asked the bellman.

"Oh, it's Germany," he answered. "The Ruhr region, where the factories are. It happens now and then. Nothing to worry about."

That was it: "Germany." This was not simply a bad odor hovering above our hotel. No, the entire city of Amsterdam was under a stinking cloud. It was like being trapped in a huge, smoke-filled room.

We were more than 100 miles west of Germany, but you could smell the stench. This prodded me to wonder about all those Germans who had lived just down the road from Dachau and other death camps sixty-five years ago. They said they had no idea what the smell was, or that Jews were being killed.... Oh, no, not a clue.

There are times when Europe reeks of the Holocaust to me. This is not because the indications are overtly present; it's my personal awareness that is heightened whenever I travel there. Even when the Holocaust is not on my mind, it creeps in, unannounced, with burning smells. Other times, I look at old buildings and wonder what went on in the dark days of World War II. I hear boots clicking on cobblestones and the shrill sounds of police sirens, and I imagine Jews being chased and captured. I walk along streets and see old people who would have been alive at that time—people who either hated the invaders or collaborated with them, who fought in the war or watched from the sidelines. Good guys who fought back, and others who surely saw or knew things but did nothing.

Many Jews in Europe chose to remain there after the war. Meeting survivors in countries where the Holocaust happened adds a painful level of poignancy that is achingly real. It's especially palpable when the weather is cold and damp, as it was in Holland for my husband and me, when spring had yet to surface with daffodils and tulips, and the earth was still buried in wintry gloom.

On this trip, we had come to attend a *bat mitzvah* in a 280-year old synagogue in den Haag. Afterward, at the *kiddish*, the 70-year old grandmother of the celebrant told me the story of her deliverance from death, which was as fresh in her mind as if it happened yesterday. Fanny was eight-years-old when the Nazis forced her, her parents, and hundreds of other Dutch Jews into a theater in Amsterdam. After days of no food or drink, Fanny was smuggled out with other children and taken to a safe home in southern Holland, where she was cared for and protected by a Catholic family.

"I never saw my parents again," she said. "I don't know how they found the courage to give me away to strangers, but it saved my life."

Fanny smiled wistfully as we looked at her two married sons and their families, especially the *bat mitzvah* girl laughing with her siblings and cousins. Then Fanny pointed to a gray-haired woman standing beside a young boy.

"She was a little girl when her parents took me in," Fanny explained. "We've stayed in touch, and I invited her today. That's her grandson with her."

A few days later, on a busy street in Amsterdam, my husband and I passed by the old theater, still in use. It was large and grand, and if you didn't know the history, you'd have no idea what had happened there. But we knew, and I could find no beauty in the building's decorative exterior, and had no desire to go inside. I could almost hear cries of anguish and terror.

We flew home to New York with stories of hope as well as of despair. At the same time we still search faces of the old with unasked questions, and stare at buildings where what is almost unspeakable happened, we also hear chronicles of such brightness and hope, and watch families that might never had existed if not for the goodness of strangers.

We are enthralled by these glimmers of light. Like young shoots of spring flowers poking up between dry autumn leaves, the stories offer us the possibilities of hope. We ride a seesaw of emotions between a haunting cloud of death and despair, and the confirmation that to save a life, you can indeed save an entire world.

The Jewish Week of New York — May 6, 2005

CHANUKAH, IN A DIFFERENT LIGHT

From a non-Jewish bank manager,
a universal blessing

"So tell me, can I light the first candle now?" asked May, my local bank manager. She pointed to an electric Chanukah menorah on a table beside a Christmas tree. All the Chanukah "candles" were in place, but none were lit. Yet.

May and I have known each other for years, ever since our now-grown kids were on baseball teams together. May is a very kind, as well as competent person, with a sunny disposition and a big heart. She also is Catholic. And I am one of her Jewish customers.

It was a Friday morning in December, 2003, and the first candle would be lit at sundown. Which is why I told May, no, she couldn't flip the switch on the bank's menorah today because they closed at 3 o'clock in the afternoon. Two more candles would be lit in Jewish homes over the weekend, so during banking hours on Monday, she should light -

"Three candles? Am I right?" she asked. Clearly, she wanted to do it correctly. I nodded yes, and explained that usually, candles are placed in the menorah from right to left, and lit from left to right, although it isn't mandatory. But I didn't say that Chanukah candles don't burn in

Jewish homes during the day, and that lighting them when she came to work in the morning, which is what she—and countless other well-intentioned managers, merchants, and employees did—was inappropriate and incorrect.

Silently, I thought, if the secular world insists on lighting menorahs, maybe they should just ignite all eight candles at once, and let it go at that. But the whole thing reminded me of the childhood game, What's Wrong with this Picture?

Also, because I knew that May's concerns were heartfelt and sincere, I didn't say that personally, I don't like seeing religious objects or symbols displayed in public places. In the same way that many Christians think the commercialization of Christmas profanes it, I agree with Jews who believe that lighting menorahs in non-Jewish settings is disrespectful. The menorah is a key religious symbol of Judaism—not the Jewish equivalent of a Christmas tree.

Christmas trees are part of the Christmas holiday, but they are not essential to it. Kindling the lights of the menorah, however, is a sacred act, central to the celebration of Chanukah. Jews, in fact, are required to do so, and we say, "We praise you, Eternal One, Source of the Universe, who teaches us holiness with your mitzvot, and commands us to kindle the Chanukah lights."

May and I talked briefly about the story of Chanukah, which commemorates the victory of the Maccabees, who crushed the mighty armies of King Antiochus Ephiphanes, in 165 B.C.E. Led by Judah Maccabee, the Jews revolted against Antiochus's campaign to destroy their faith by banning the study of Torah, demanding that Jews worship idols, and deliberately desecrating their Temple by sacrificing pigs on the altar.

After the Temple was cleansed and rebuilt, oil was collected and lit in candelabras. Part of the story of Chanukah describes the "miracle of the oil which lasted eight days instead of one," but the primary message focuses on resisting assimilation into the mainstream, no matter how much pressure there is in some cases, or how attractive and tantalizing it may be in others.

"Celebrate and rejoice with mirth and gladness," said Judah Maccabee. But there was something else -

"By the way," I told May, "we don't just light candles."

She looked at me quizzically.

"We recite a blessing in Hebrew," I explained. "It's fundamental in Judaism to do an act and say a blessing, in that order."

Her shoulders slumped. Was she sorry she had started this?

"But I can't recite a Hebrew blessing," she replied.

I agreed. But we both knew that saying nothing was not the answer.

"Surely, you can recite something, May," I said. "Some sort of universal prayer—for peace, good health, and love."

She smiled. "Of course, I can," she said.

I smiled back and thought, Okay, I can live with that.

The Jewish Week of New York — December 3, 2004

SETTLEMENT HOUSE SPIRIT LIVES ON

If you look closely above the front door of Manhattan Comprehensive Night and Day High School, you can see the acronym "HTSG" carved in stone. The letters stand for Hebrew Technical School for Girls, which my grandmother Etta attended in the early 1900s, when it was located on the Lower East Side. The new building, still standing at 240 Second Avenue, was constructed in 1906.

How a school established for poor Jewish girls became a refuge for today's immigrant students and high-school dropouts in search of a second chance is a story of both a changing city and a legacy of a visionary era in Jewish philanthropy.

The school was founded in 1880 by Minnie Dessau Louis, a journalist, philanthropist and stalwart of the city's premier Reform temple, Emanu-El. Louis first established the school on the top floor of a building on East Broadway, giving lessons in personal hygiene and religion to thirty girls from needy Jewish immigrant families on the Lower East Side. A few years later, the Louis Down-Town Sabbath School moved to Henry Street and expanded its curriculum to include courses in English, ethics, arithmetic, bookkeeping, typewriting, sewing, physical education and biblical history.

Renamed Hebrew Technical School for Girls in 1895, the school was backed by devoted teachers and a board of directors dedicated to the belief that "for those who need help, there is nothing better than to help them help themselves." Instruction was free, supported by philanthropic donations from wealthy "uptown" Jews, including Adolph Lewisohn, Jacob Schiff and Felix Warburg.

In 1906, a brand-new, fireproof, five-story building was opened at 240 Second Ave. with an auditorium, gymnasium, running track, cafeteria and library, as well as classrooms. Locker rooms and a swimming pool could even be found on the basement level.

In an era when few girls received educations beyond grammar school, visionaries such as Nathaniel Myers, Hebrew Tech's long-term president, recognized that "the best way to extend life-long help to needy and deserving young girls was to educate them to become self-respecting, self-supporting, progressive and ambitious." Most entering students were 14-years-old enrolled in a two-year curriculum of courses. By 1909, nearly two-thirds of some 400 students were in the commercial program learning office skills; the rest focused on manual subjects such as millinery and dressmaking.

My grandmother was fortunate to be a student. She acquired skills that kept her out of punishing sweatshops and enabled her to earn good wages as a bookkeeper.

Hebrew Tech closed its doors in 1932, but its mission continued. The board set up a foundation providing financial aid to disadvantaged young women seeking higher education. Today, it continues to award grants and loans, on a nonsectarian basis, as the Manhattan-based Jewish Foundation for Education of Women (*www.jfew.*

org). As Jenna Weissman Joselit put it in <u>Aspiring Women</u>, her 1996 history of the foundation, "Pink-collar workers in elaborately trimmed hats have given way to corporate lawyers in blue serge suits, while immigrants from Beijing have taken the place of those from Belarus. And yet, surely, Minnie Louis would feel right at home at one of the Scholarship Committee's Monday-morning meetings."

The sturdy school building was purchased by the New York City Board of Education, and for the next fifty-seven years, it was used as an annex for trade and vocational schools.

In 1989, however, something remarkable happened. Howard Friedman, formerly a public school teacher, obtained a grant to found a new school in the Hebrew Tech building for foreign-born and previously "at-risk" young adults between the ages of seventeen and twenty-two. Many were high school dropouts who had lost their ways temporarily, for a variety of complicated and overwhelming reasons. Others were new immigrants who spoke little or no English. They were too old, or their lives were too fractured by jobs and family obligations, to attend conventional schools. But Manhattan Comprehensive Night and Day High School would give them the chance to earn academic diplomas and to advance to college and graduate study. More than a century after Louis dedicated herself to the education of poor girls and immigrants, her cause has been given new life.

Today, Manhattan Comprehensive is funded by grants, private donations and the Board of Education. It serves more than 800 students, with a graduation rate of more than 90%. The school is open year-round, seven days a week, until 10:45 most evenings, to accommodate students' outside responsibilities. Roughly 35% have children to support. The Student Life Center provides assistance for job counseling and referrals, housing aid, legal problems, medical care and personal guidance. Volunteers from private and public sectors help students with English, SAT preparation, math, science and history. The need for volunteers is great.

No doubt, few of today's students notice Louis's name inscribed in the marble of the lobby wall or the old brass plaques commemorating Hebrew Tech. But they probably would appreciate the words in my grandmother's schoolgirl autograph album:

"I trust that your success here may be a stepping-stone to successes in your future," wrote Mary Lindsay, one of my grandmother's teachers.

Her friend Rose wrote: "There may be times when you cannot find help. But there is no time when you cannot give help."

Henrietta, another classmate, counseled, "In the tempest of life, when the wave and the gale /Are around and above, if thy footing should fail /If thine eye should grow dim, and thy caution depart /Look aloft and be firm, and be fearless of heart."

The Jewish Forward — May 11, 2001

KEYS
TO
HOME

Best-ever Gordon Halloween pumpkin!

THE KEY TO HOME

When I look at childhood pictures of my older brother and me, taken in the 1950s, I see a blond haired boy with glasses and a girl with curly brown hair, holding hands and squinting toward the camera. Nearby is our red brick apartment house. Over the years, the trees which shaded it grew taller, and their leaves changed color with the seasons, but the house looks the same in every picture—a shy bystander, watching us. We never thought of stepping aside and taking a picture of this ordinary building. But now I find myself staring at photos of this place which became my home when my mother left my father, their suburban house, and what she emphatically declared was their "miserable marriage." I was two-years-old and my brother Jerry was almost seven when we moved into my grandmother's small apartment in Queens, and stayed for the rest of my childhood.

My father hated my grandmother for taking us in, and he hated my mother for leaving him. Mainly, he took his feelings of rage and frustration out on my brother and me, especially during court-ordered visitations. "You're *my* children and you belong in *my* house!" he'd howl, smacking his fist on the dashboard of his car as we sped down the block, away from Grandma's home.

Her "junior four" apartment had only one bedroom. My crib and two beds were jammed into it, and Grandma began sleeping on the living room studio couch. Space was tight, but my mother soon found a job and was out all day, and Grandma tolerated the distinctive mess made by Jerry and me. Toy trains crisscrossed the living room rug, coloring books fanned out on table tops, dolls lounged on chairs, and shoeboxes filled with puzzle pieces, crayons and baseball cards piled up everywhere. Even the bathroom door was never shut. "What's to hide?" asked Grandma. "We're all family here."

Life had a calm predictability in Grandma's home except when angry battles between my parents erupted with Vesuvian force as they fought about everything including her going back to him ("Never!") to his paying child support ("I'm broke don't you know?") In the stormy family stew that was my almost-daily diet, the fights went on for years, and exacerbated the agonizing stress of visitations that Jerry and I were forced to endure. Neighbors often overheard the commotion and tittered about it interminably. For a long time, we were the laughing-stock of the building.

Eight six-story buildings in the Queens Gardens Apartments where we lived comprised an entire city block in Rego Park. More than half the property was set aside for play areas and gardens, which pleased the middle-class tenants who had come from jam-packed urban dwellings. There were grassy areas with park benches under cherry trees laden with fat pink blossoms in the springtime, and maple trees that separated the sidewalks from the curbs. Black wrought iron fences rimmed the children's playground, preventing toddlers from wandering away from their mothers, who sat on benches, rocking baby carriages. Parents leaned out of upstairs windows to watch their children and toss down sweaters if it got cool, or drop money wrapped in wads of paper napkins for ice cream when the Good Humor truck came by.

From the rooftops, where mothers hung wash on clotheslines in the summertime while their children peered breathlessly over the stone parapets, you could see traffic on Queens Boulevard wind its way west, past Horace Harding Boulevard, vacant lots, shops and other buildings in Elmhurst, Corona, Sunnyside and Long Island City, until you saw the faint curves and filigreed outline of the Queensborough Bridge which spanned the East River and separated Queens from Manhattan.

Each apartment building had its own entrance, and was connected to the others by lengthy, underground networks of corridors with whitewashed walls. Eddie-the-Assistant-Superintendent lived with his family in a basement apartment with windows that looked up at the sidewalk. Their front door was painted red and their green concrete "front yard" was edged by a white picket fence and gate that Eddie had constructed. He was a sweet man who fixed leaky faucets and toilets, put up screens in the summer, and helped my grandmother maintain our home.

We were not like other families in the building. No father came home at night with his hat tipped back, tie loosened, and newspaper tucked under his arm, and no mother ever waited by the door to greet him. My friends' fathers weren't around after school, but there was a maleness about their homes, even those furnished with flowery curtains and upholstery. Men's bulky coats dominated hall closets, and shaving brushes and scented creams commandeered space on bathroom sinks. Neckties hung on bedroom doorknobs, and wooden pipes lounged in ashtrays beside pouches of smoking tobacco. I remember seeing a pair of men's black galoshes on a closet floor. One galosh stood straight, but the other had slumped over, and nuzzled against a woman's boot.

I have no photographs of my grandmother cooking or cleaning, kneading pie dough with her arthritic fingers or bending over the bathtub to rub my back with a warm soapy washcloth. There is no picture of my mother rising before dawn to shower and dress before she left our apartment and dashed for the subway station five blocks away, where she caught a train for her job downtown. Nor is there a picture of the dressing table where she sat and transformed herself, before my eyes, from a pretty woman into a most beautiful one. But I can see these people, and the rooms they occupied, as clearly as if they were pictures in an album. Slowly, in my mind, I enter the front door and wander through the rooms. I see where every piece of furniture stood, and how the sunlight shifted from our living room windows in the morning, to the bedroom and kitchen windows late in the day. Photographs really aren't necessary when I think about home.

My mother remarried when I was a teenager, and our new family moved to Long Island. "Keep your key," Grandma told me. "Never forget, you can always come back."

I returned often, for weekend visits or just for dinner. Being part of a new family was exciting but stressful. My stepfather was nice, but it took a long time for me to get to know him, and even longer before I fell in love with him. Also, things had changed between my mother and me, because most of her attention was directed towards her job, my stepfather, and the energies it took for them to make their marriage work. When my grandmother died, during my junior year in college, I knew that I had lost my beloved best friend.

Straightaway, my mother and I went to Grandma's apartment to sort and throw out most of her things. Hastily, we dumped pots and pans, dishes, mixing bowls, knick-knacks, sheets and towels down the incinerator chute because it was torture to be there, emptying this apartment so full of the past, so full of all the years I had spent there as a child. We told Eddie's wife to take whatever she wanted, and made phone calls to charities and dealers of secondhand goods to get rid of the remaining clothes and shabby furniture. All we saved were some framed prints, one lamp, my grandmother's books, jewelry, and her photographs.

Nothing was deemed to have value, although I suspect that it did. The furniture was worn but it was solidly built, and some of it was beautiful. I never enter a thrift shop or antiques store without looking for my grandmother's belongings. Maybe I'll find the mahogany drum table with the scalloped pie-crust edge I liked to "dust" with my fingers, the red Chinese chest decorated with painted birds, the pink marble coffee table with wrought iron roses twirling around the base, the ornate bedroom set and gilt-edged mirrors.

After the last closet and drawer were emptied, and all the shelves were bare, my mother and I left Grandma's apartment and locked the door. I tucked my key into my pocket; how could I throw it away? It's been on my keychain ever since, hanging beside keys to other apartments, including those my husband and I rented during the first years of our marriage, and the house we purchased when our sons were young.

Twenty-one years after Grandma died, my stepfather died, too. Heading back from the cemetery, my husband, sons and I passed through my old neighborhood. All of us were heart-sick and shaken, but somehow this seemed like the right time for me to go home. For a long time after Grandma died, I had purposeful avoided walking down her street, and turned my head away whenever I drove by. My entire childhood, her eyes had fallen on me like a sweet benediction when she kissed me goodbye as I headed for school or my father's waiting car. I couldn't accept seeing other lights turned on in her home, or someone else watching from her windows.

Now, as my family and I approached the building, I scanned the ground floor windows of her apartment. It was vacant, except for a wooden ladder and cans of paint on the kitchen floor. We entered the lobby, and I reached into my handbag for Grandma's key. Of course, it didn't fit in the lock.

"Goodbye," I whispered, touching my old front door gently. I remembered times when I had played in the living room and Grandma would say she was tired, and go lie down on my brother's bed. After a while, I'd tiptoe into the darkened bedroom. I'd stand there, worried, motionless and quiet, as still as an empty hanger in an empty closet, and I would stare at Grandma to make sure she was breathing. Without her, what would have happened to us? How could my mother have worked and taken care of us too?

The last time I had been in Grandma's bedroom was soon after she had died. I was taking a respite from the numbing task of throwing things away when a late afternoon sunbeam peeked through the curtains and settled on a strand of Grandma's silky white hair. It was fine and fragile, and as tiny as an eyelash. I pressed my fingertip against it and picked it up. For a moment, I held it in the palm of my hand. Then I placed it on my tongue and swallowed it.

Now, in the lobby of my childhood home, I looked at my husband and sons and knew that I loved them as completely as Grandma had loved me. We walked outside and looked through the windows again. Then I reached into my handbag and clutched the only key I really needed, the key to our present home.

First published here, in <u>Counting Heads</u> — 2023

A NEW HOME
FOR THE HOLIDAYS

I live in a house built in 1931. Construction began soon after the start of the Great Depression, but by the time the house was finished, the builder couldn't sell it, so he lived there for nine years. Since 1940, just three families have owned the house. The shortest duration was seven years, when a job transfer compelled the family before us to move out quickly. The husband departed first, leaving his understandably overwhelmed wife to pack up everything including their three kids, pet hamster, pet monkey, and tropical fish aquarium.

We moved in shortly before Thanksgiving, and were determined to host a real holiday celebration. Until then, we'd lived in different city apartments. but now we planned to make this place our home for a long time. Amid the jumbled chaos of packing crates and unwieldy wads of Bubble Wrap, we dug into boxes to extricate the gravy boat, candlesticks, cranberry spoon, favorite bowl-that-always-holds-the-stuffing, and—from one of my late mother-in-law's Thanksgiving-time birthday cakes—the tiny plastic turkey that has stood proudly atop the dessert every year. Even today, my personal thoughts about Thanksgiving center on that first year, when a new beginning confirmed that we had come home.

One year, my sons Edward and Peter decorated the dining room with joyful paintings of orange turkeys with blue, yellow, and purple feathers, and red wattles dangling from scraggy necks. In one picture, seven-year old Peter had drawn a turkey standing by our house and saying "Wellkom!" The grandparents loved everything, of course, and praised the remarkable talents of "the young Rembrandts."

So far, four generations of boys-only have grown up in our house. This has meant a great deal of tumbling down the stairs (necessitating habitual repair of the banisters and newel posts), hide-and-seek games, "friendly" wrestling bouts, toy rocket launchings, miniature car races, and indoor hockey (don't ask!) During the winter months, when school and work schedules required waking up before sunrise and returning home in darkness in late afternoon, the children played indoors even more. But the house always seemed to graciously expand to suit our needs.

It's a lovely house, with leaded-glass windows, recessed alcoves, and secluded nooks rarely found in newer dwellings. The sounds and smells are familiar and comforting to us. We know which treads will creak beneath our feet on the staircase, which doors stick in muggy weather, and which radiators hiss whenever the heat goes on. Home is where you can find your way in the dark.

There are no veritable ghosts, but subtle intimations of the past persist. Mysterious breezes awaken old memories whenever a late-afternoon sunbeam strikes, for a moment, a once beloved Matchbox car or pinpoints the cracked spine of child's picture book on an out-of-the-way shelf. Is it an apparition that gently stirs the air beside me, bringing back faint scents of baby powder that almost take my breath away?

Home is a place where you live as a child, and then carry with you the rest of your life. In her autobiography, <u>Blackberry Winter</u>, world-renowned anthropologist Margaret Mead spoke about the basic need we have to set up semblances of "home," no matter where we are, or how many years have gone by. "In all my years of field work," Mead wrote, "each small object I have brought with me, each arrangement on a shelf of tin cans holding beads... or crayons for the children to draw with become the mark of home.... " So can a child's painting.

Many years after that first Thanksgiving celebration, and soon after Peter left for college, he casually remarked, "I don't live home any more." My husband and I were visiting Peter in St. Louis, and until that moment, I thought all three of us were away from our family's home in New York. Now, I was hearing something else (not, "I don't live at home now.")

His tone was cheerful and matter-of-fact. He's a terrific son, and I knew he didn't mean to hurt our feelings, so I smiled as brightly as possible, and said, "Right." But silently, I thought, *Peter, you may change, but home never does.* And I fought the urge to add, no matter where you go, or what you do, our home will always be there for you... to return to, whenever you wish—even if sometimes all it might be is a small private place in a corner of your mind.

My husband and I flew back home the next day, and kept in touch with Peter. He shared stories of new friends and classes, but I couldn't forget his unintentionally bruising words. In mid-November, I started gathering things to use on Thanksgiving Day. When I came across the "Wellkom" picture, I knew it was time to hang it up again.

A few days later, Peter called from St. Louis. "I'm coming home, Mom. I'll be there on Wednesday."

"Right," I said again. And once more, I smiled brightly.

Victoria — November/December 2013

IRE RISES AS LEAVES COME DOWN

There is a small war going on, on my street. It may explode into armed combat (I, with my one-woman powered hand rake and he, with his five-horse-powered leaf blower) if a certain gardener doesn't mend—or perhaps I should say, cultivate—his ways.

Except during the blissfully peaceful months of January and February, I hear his rackety truck rattle and sputter down my street each Tuesday afternoon. Although he works for the family next door, Joe the gardener always parks in front of my house, his mud-caked wheels aggressively shoving the carefully placed rocks I use to separate my lawn from the street. "Look, lady," he replies when I ask him to please move his truck, "this is city property, and I got a right to park here if I wanna."

In the spring and summer, he mows my neighbor's lawn, and for close to an hour my nose and ears are assaulted by the stench of gasoline and the raucous clamor of machinery. But the sound of the mower is dulcet—practically symphonic—compared with the deafening roar of his cleanup tool, the blowing machine he uses to collect all the grass clippings.

The day Joe comes, my neighbor goes out. She can't bear the noise, she tells me, and regularly schedules her art classes for that particular time. My routine is different, however; I work at home, and the only time I have is between the hours of 9 a.m. and 3 p.m., when my children are at school.

Like most writers, I need quiet—a precious commodity in a noisy household. When the kids depart, I settle down, blessing the easy calm of the day before me. But Joe has arrived with his machinery, and the blatant barrage of backfires, bangs, booms and crashes sends uncontrollable tremors through my typewriter tapping fingers. What a way to sabotage literary success!

Autumn, as every homeowner knows, is "Cleanup Time." The leaves come down in mad, messy abandon and scatter themselves over everyone's lawn with no respect for property lines, fences or other artificial barriers. Joe arrives early on Fall Cleanup Days and, with a fanaticism for spotlessness that no housemaid of mine ever briefly entertained, attacks my neighbor's lawn with Draconian zeal. No leaf, no twig or branch which isn't firmly attached to a living plant will remain by the time he is finished. Back and forth he marches, his muscular arms pushing his giant mowing machine, a menacing contraption that tempestuously sends all the clutter out to the street edge.

Getting things out of the bushes is a more difficult but not insurmountable job. Now he blows with a smaller, hand-held tube whose power unit is strapped to his back. Brazenly, he allows the bulk of his curbside collection to "drift" on to my lawn. I run outside to nab him. "Aha," I announce, "you are caught in the act! How dare you blow your leaves onto my lawn?"

"What do you mean, *my* leaves, Mrs.?" he answers. (He has never learned my name, and doesn't choose to ask for it. I, and the rest of his noncustomers, are simply called by our prefixes.) "The leaves, they can blow anywhere. I cannot help it if they go to your lawn." He grins obsequiously. "You did not see me place them there, did you?" His hand is extended, palm up. He turns it over toward the ground, to clarify the word, "place."

I wonder, do all gardeners behave like this? Perhaps they have a pact—each week they purposely blow leaves on to each other's lawns, so everyone will have something to clean up on his next visit.

My friend five miles away tells me the gardeners in her neighborhood aren't much better. She's been eyeing one crafty character for several years, and this is what she reports: Residents in her town pile their leaves by the street edges of their lawns, where city-owned garbage trucks regularly collect the debris. One gardener won't leave his customers with a sloppy curbside, however, and since he can't let all the leaves "drift" into the street, he gathers them up in a large burlap sack and carries them, Santa Claus-style, down the block. There, in a warped gesture of generosity, he deposits them on someone else's leaf pile!

No one, we are convinced, uses bamboo rakes anymore, or catch-all bags on the backs of their mowers, except people like us—people without gardeners. And although we maintain our lawns quietly, with the slow steady sounds of people-powered hand clippers, lawn mowers and leaf rakers, we are the auditory, olfactory and emotional victims of maniacs who drive machine-operated lawn-care equipment.

The New York Times — October 25, 1981

ONE ACT REDEFINES 'NEIGHBOR'

This is a Thanksgiving kind of story, although it took place almost two weeks before that lovely holiday. It happened on one of those cold and overcast days in late autumn, a time when the sun sets by late afternoon, and sometimes a darkness of the spirit, as well as of the sky, can settle in around us quite suddenly.

An unexpected brightness appeared in my life, and in the life of my teen-age son, Peter. The brightness came from a neighbor named Loretta, someone we hardly knew.

Loretta and her family live two blocks away. Whenever we pass each other in our cars, or in one of the local stores, we smile the polite smile of people who live near each other but don't know each other very well. We're neighbors, but we've never been close. Last November, however, Loretta appeared out of nowhere, and lent me a big helping hand I will never forget. Her simple gesture of friendship and concern made me realize that the network of people I could count on in a pinch was much larger that what I had imagined.

Last fall, Peter began his final season on his high school's ice hockey team. He was not a star player. In fact, it took huge efforts of practice and training for him to be any good at all. Furthermore, when he started two years earlier, he could barely skate.

"I'll practice and I'll learn," he had asserted at that time, and he handed me a parents' consent form from school.

"I can't believe I'm signing this," I sighed. "My kid—playing a killer sport like ice hockey." He had always been such a sweet-tempered boy. Did our family genes contain some ancient Canadian bloodline I didn't know about? Maybe they did, because Peter played his hardest, and by the end of the first season, he had earned the award for Most Improved Player.

But my story focuses on his last year, when he advanced to the varsity level. Now he would enjoy all the benefits of playing in the big league—decent ice time for practice, a complete (and matching) uniform, and the glories of victory we hoped would soon be his. The fourth day of practice, he called me from a phone booth at the ice rink. "I twisted my ankle badly," he said. "And I think I broke it. I've got to get to the emergency room fast." He had taken our car to the rink earlier, and since he had injured his left foot, he said he could drive to the hospital by himself. "I'll meet you there as soon as I can," I told him, and hung up. First, I called a close friend, who lives across the street, confident she'd be able to drive me to the hospital. But she had a house full of three-year-olds. "My day to run the playgroup," she explained over the din. "There's no way I can get out of here." Next, I called another neighbor, but she wasn't home. Then I tried a local taxi service. "How fast can you come to the intersection of Avondale Road and Ridgeway?" I asked the dispatcher on the phone. "Not for fifteen minutes at best," he answered. It was getting close to dinnertime and most of his drivers had either gone home or were meeting commuter trains at the railroad station. "I've no one else to ask," I told him, "so send me a cab."

In the brief meantime, I reached for the phone book and called three orthopedists I knew, hoping to take Peter to one of their offices and avoid consulting with an unknown emergency-room doctor. But everyone had already left for the day.

It was getting late, but I still had about eight minutes. I grabbed a coat and left my house. Running down the street, I scolded myself for arranging to meet the cab at my corner. Then I saw it go by—seven minutes early and in a hurry. I was only halfway down the block but I kept on going, hoping the driver would turn around and come back. My kid was hurt and I couldn't get to him. Should I run to the main street and wait for a bus, I wondered, or go back home and call for another cab?

An unfamiliar car appeared and slowed down. Someone rolled down a window and stared at me. It was Loretta, the neighbor I barely knew.

"Are you all right?" she called out. Although it was quite cold, I was still holding my coat in my hands, and I must have looked as dazed on the outside as I was feeling inside.

"I've got to get to the hospital right away," I told her. "My son's in the emergency room."

"Get in," she said, and I did. Quickly, she backed her car into the nearest driveway and turned around. "He'll be fine," she said consolingly. "You'll see, everything will be all right."

We reached the hospital in minutes, which was a blessing because the medical staff would do nothing for Peter until I showed up and signed the necessary forms.

As crises go, this one wasn't too bad. Peter's ankle had suffered a clean break, with no tiny shards of bone or torn ligaments to complicate things and require surgery. The next day, when he was stretched out on the sofa with his foot in a cast, I thought about Loretta, and how much gratitude I felt. Where had she been going when she said I should get in her car? What matters did she unselfishly—and unhesitatingly—postpone?

Most of us know we can count on our families and our very dear friends. They're supposed to drop everything when we're in trouble. But there are other people—people we're not close to, neighbors who live nearby but never enter our homes, co-workers and shopkeepers whom we see every day but don't confide in, that string of people on the fringe of our relationships—whose support is also there for us, when and if we need it.

Sooner or later, most of us are rescued by people like Loretta. Our car runs out of gas and someone we barely know appears out of the blue and takes us to a gas station. Or we gasp on the lane at the supermarket after the checker has rung up all our groceries, when we realize we left our wallet home; and then a neighbor taps us on the shoulder and saves the day with some ready cash. Sooner or later, we find ourselves breathing a big sigh of relief. And a sigh of thanks.

Thanks, Loretta.

The New York Times — November 20, 1988

IN THE GARDEN

In early March, after months reading gardening magazines, and studying our landscape through windows sealed against the cold, I begin venturing outside not simply to retrieve the newspaper or climb into my car, but to breathe crisp fresh air, and think about spring.

I barely can abide the first weeks, still damp, gloomy, and dispiriting as I seek subtle signs of the coming season. Then one day, a robin alights on a frozen patch of lawn in my yard. "Look! We Have Come Through!" I think, recalling the words of poet D. H. Lawrence.

The robin's head darts swiftly, left—right—left—right; open areas are never entirely safe for a little bird. But the ground provides good vantage points to search for food or scout out locations for a nest. He jabs his beak into a clump of leaves that have been whipped together by high winds and storms. I know I must not move, not even from the sheltered and appreciable distance of my back door; the slightest tremor and he'll take wing. But after a long, dreary winter, my eyes and heart must savor the uplifting arrival of this optimistic, hopeful bird.

It must be a male robin, because they migrate first, to establish their domains. Within weeks, he will be joined by a spirited female attracted by his merry call. They will build their nest with dry grasses, leaves, twigs, and twine and pack it together snugly with mud. She does most of the construction, while her mate gathers the materials and watches for predators. He will not sing near the nest during egg-laying or incubation time, lest he gives away its location. Everything is done for good reason; robins instinctively position their nests to face south and east, ensuring sunshine and warmth in the mornings, and shady afternoons on hot summer days.

Nature has its plans and patterns, no matter what we want or expect. But it's a pleasure to adjust to the lengthening days and melting snow. As the ground thaws, rock-hard dirt turns oozy and wet and thoughts of new beginnings seep into our winter-hardened pores. This is when the world is "mud-luscious" and "puddle-wonderful," which is how the poet e.e.cummings described it. I love the scent of skunk cabbage, often the first green plant to push through snow and ice. Although the cabbage's odor is unpleasant, its pungency is a potent wake-up call, and the heat generated by its unfolding leaves attracts swarms of bees to pollinate its flowers.

I'm glad that I planted bulbs in the fall. I had postponed the task for weeks, waiting for a sunny, not-too-cold day, until I realized I was running out of time. My rewards now are green shoots poking up from the ground, followed by a happy parade of snowdrops, jonquils, and muscari. Lavender, white, and purple crocuses pop up totally out of place in the middle of the lawn, like amusing, unexpected gifts. Later bulbs, such as tulips and hyacinths, may be grander and more glorious, but the sight of early flowers is the most energizing tonic.

As usual, I will plant annuals and vegetables, although I might get lazy and see what grows unexpectedly. Years ago, my family always planted pumpkin seeds with great care, setting them into the soil at just the right depth, watering regularly, and gently tilling the dirt around them. First, two small oval leaves would emerge, followed by vigorous green vines, larger and prickly leaves, and trumpet-shaped orange-yellow flowers. After a while, the flowers would be pollinated by bees and be replaced by grape-sized green balls. These, we knew, were little pumpkins-in-the-making.

"Great!" we'd cheer; this year we will have pumpkins for pies as well as Halloween decorations. But then the plants would be attacked either by mildew or insects, and the vines would wither and die. Our tomatoes, beans, onions, beets, peppers and eggplants thrived. But we had no luck growing pumpkins. So we quit.

"No pumpkins this year," I announced to my dismayed sons. "It's a waste of time. Why plant them and be let down again? I'd rather just take you to the farmer's market to pick out your pumpkins; it's what we always end up doing, anyway."

The boys were disappointed, but they knew I was right. Together, we accepted the harsh reality: not everything you plant will grow, no matter how good your intentions (and hard work).

That summer, as I was spreading mulch in our vegetable garden, I noticed some undistinguished green foliage that looked vaguely familiar. Was this a tiny pumpkin plant? I continued to work, doing my best to ignore the plant, and paid scant attention to it until early September ... when I no longer could ignore the fact that a sturdy orange pumpkin was growing where none had survived before!

Most likely, it had sprouted from a dormant, left-over seed from the previous year, or else it was the stalwart "fruit" of one of those spindly, pathetic grape-sized balls that had plunked to the ground in exhaustion. With no tending, no cultivation, no pinching back, and no rotating of the pumpkin to keep it symmetrical in shape, it had come up and thrived on its own accord.

You probably have figured out the rest. By October 1st, it was clear that we would, indeed, have a home-grown Jack O'Lantern. Our unblemished pumpkin was perfectly round and gorgeously fat. If it were larger, it could have been Cinderella's coach!

Looking back, I realize there must have been two or more blossoms on that determined vine, because bees need at least two flowers to perform pollination. In any case, only one pumpkin flourished. What I do recall, for certain, was the awesome recognition that forces greater than our gardening skills had been at work. Even though we didn't plant a pumpkin vine, Nature had decided to do it.

Victoria — March/April 2009

HOMEWORK IN APLACE THAT'S NOT HOME

Three afternoons a week, about twenty-five children living temporarily at the Coachman Hotel in White Plains, New York come to its Homework Center after school. Five years ago, the Coachman was an ordinary hotel, but now the people who live there aren't ordinary guests.

There are security guards at the front desk, instead of reservations clerks. The carpet is worn and shabby, the walls are soiled, and two microwave ovens are on a table in the lobby. There's no park nearby, so mothers and babies sit outside by the parking lot. The Coachman Hotel is home for the homeless.

At the Homework Center, in two rooms off the lobby that had been used as offices, volunteer tutors help the children with their schoolwork. Many volunteers are retirees, or employed people who can take a few hours off. Others are high school students and former teachers.

I've been helping out at the center for more than a year. We offer the children snacks, a quiet place to work, and grown-ups who can give them undivided attention. Ideally, each child would be tutored by one volunteer, but there are never enough of us. And yet, most days, a great deal gets accomplished. The children read stories, draw pictures and do math. They work on puzzles, play word games and learn how to measure distances. We've gotten supplies from schools, religious organizations, office-supply companies and private contributors. Everything is kept in file cabinets, along with progress reports about the children. Last week, a volunteer noted, a sixth-grade boy got his first library card.

Working at the Coachman gives me plenty to think about: What does the word, "homework" mean to a homeless child? Why do Federal Government policies provide money only for temporary housing, not for anything permanent? And if this hotel is meant for "temporary" housing, why are most of the children I knew last year still here? I asked one boy where he lived before. "Yonkers Motel," he told me. That was "temporary," too.

When the children arrive at the center, they toss their coats on chairs and head right for the snacks. They're not always ready to begin work. After all, they've just spent a full day in school, and many have traveled a long way to get here.

Some of the children come in taxicabs from schools in Peekskill, Yonkers and other parts of the county. Others go to school in White Plains, and they travel on school buses, just like the other kids. But instead of being dropped off at their homes, these children go to the Coachman.

It's no surprise that some days, they can't sit still. They're restless and impatient, and they pester each other. By the time five o'clock arrives, everyone is exhausted. Even so, this time is never wasted. If one child learns one thing, then it has all been worth it.

"How was your day?" a volunteer asks a first grader who is sipping apple juice and munching on a graham cracker.

The little girl sighs and says, "It was okay." Her hair is braided into intricate fine rows, but her shoes are too big for her feet. She shows the volunteer some worksheets and they sit down together to work. On the floor, four children play Scrabble with a high school student. Another volunteer places two very young children on her lap, and reads them a story. Other children drop in for a while, to see what's doing. If there were more volunteers to show an interest in them, I'm sure these children would stay.

"I was once homeless," a high school volunteer tells a nine-year-old boy. "My house burned down a few years ago. We lost all our things. My cat died, too. It was awful."

"My house burned down in Mount Vernon," the younger child replies. "Now I go to school in White Plains. But I don't like it. I can't see my friends."

"I know what you mean," the volunteer says. "I was very angry for a long time. My family and I had to move into a motel. It was horrible there. I had a lot of anger. But then I realized that school was the best part of my day. And that's where I put all my energies." He's a senior now and in the National Honor Society. Last year, his family found another home. Things do work out, sometimes.

It's been said that people become homeless because of drug abuse, alcohol problems or simply because of something they have done. It's painful to think of these things when I look at the children of the Coachman. They are not responsible for any of their problems. In fact, they are very good kids dealing extremely well with a terrible situation. Some of them have serious learning difficulties, but others are very bright.

Will they be able to climb out of this mess some day? Can we help them put all their energies into their schoolwork as the high school volunteer has? It would be wonderful if none of us had to come here anymore, if all the children were in real homes again, and this hotel were filled with tour groups and wedding parties.

It's almost 5 p.m. We're getting ready to close. Supplies and projects are put back into the cabinets. "Where are you going now?" a small boy asks me as we're walking toward the door. I swallow hard and answer. "Well, I'm going home.'

The New York Times — April 22, 1990

SOME HELPFUL GARDENING HINTS FOR SUBURBAN TRANSPLANTS

Before I moved to the suburbs, the only clinging vines I knew were long-fingernailed girls at fraternity parties. Before I moved to the suburbs, snails were served in six-sectioned dishes by snooty French waiters—they didn't squish under my feet after a rainstorm.

I worried about halitosis—not chlorosis. And the only woodpecker I knew was "Woody," who never used my rain gutters to signal his friends at four a.m. What did I need to know about gardening? Grass was anything green that covered the ground. But, like many newcomers to suburban life, I bought a house and it came with a yard. Work had to be done, and there was no way I could avoid it.

Unless you have the courage to cover the grounds of your property with green cement, and paint bushes and flowers all around the base of your house, some time and money must be spent regularly outside the house on gardening. This bucolic term—"gardening"—may evoke images of ladies with bonnets wearing little green-thumbed gloves kneeling before radiantly healthy flower beds, but that picture is far from realistic. I'm talking about basic lawn care here. I'm talking about mowing lawns, trimming hedges, raking leaves and shoveling compost.

Families rarely garden together. Children, in fact, may fool you when they're in nursery school, merrily singing "Carrots grow from carrot seeds" and happily cultivating sweet potato plants in jelly jars. It's a good beginning, you'll think; when they're older, what terrific helpers they'll be!

But by the time they're eight or nine, a dramatic shift in their attentions will occur: the lawn will be useful only for soccer, softball and basketball practices. You ask them to grow something? Water something? No way! That would mess up their playing fields! (This period of sports enthusiasm will end quite suddenly when your children reach the age of sixteen. At that time, the only part of your property that will attract them will be your driveway, on which they'll come and go, in the family car.)

Husbands are strong—although unreliable—gardening helpers. If the Yankees, Jets or Knicks aren't on television, these spouses will probably want to get some exercise. Unfortunately, ever since some physical-fitness nuts convinced our male population that the best ways to work off excess pounds was by jogging, bicycling and participating in other nonproductive activities, "yard duty" became a thing of the past.

Try as we may to avoid it, some of us must care for our outdoor property. The following is a list describing the most common topics of gardening life:

BUGS are tiny living creatures who work, play and have sex on your property, rent free. Despite many statements by gardening "experts," no bugs are "good" bugs just because they eat "bad" bugs. Most of them would just as soon take a bite out of you or me. Verily, the only "good" bug is a dead bug.

SHRUBS are green plants that grow around the outside of the house. There are basically three kinds of shrubs—round, square and pointed. When landscaping, it's important to select a good mix of shapes. For example, "square, round, round, square" is better balanced than "square, round pointed, pointed," and not as monotonous as "square, square, square, square."

Before you dash off to the nursery to buy shrubs, be warned that they must be watered, pruned and periodically sprayed with bug spray if they are to survive and (hopefully) grow, and that they have an incredible knack for dying within two weeks after the nursery's warranty expires. Some homeowners having a run of bad horticultural luck should consider hanging dollar bills from the branches of their dead bushes, and not invest more money in new plantings. The look will still be green, but it will cost less and never need watering, pruning or spraying.

GRASS is anything green that covers the ground.

FLOWERS are small, colorful plants used to decorate the garden. There are three ways to "grow" flowers. The oldest method involves growing them from seed. Ambitious gardeners begin their flower gardens in January, covering dining room tables, window sills, bookshelves and other immobile objects in their homes with empty cake tins, margarine tubs and cottage cheese containers full of sterilized soil and seeds. Other gardeners, looking for more timesaving methods, buy their seedlings at garden centers in early spring.

The most simple (and, in the long run, most economical) way to have an easy-to-care-for colorful garden is to spend about twenty bucks on a large assortment of plastic flowers that can be stuck in the ground at random or in carefully arranged patterns. Want a few "clippings" for indoor vases? No problem. Pull out a few beauties and make a bouquet. When it starts to look dusty, you can "replant" it outside. Just remember to bring everything in by late fall; only crocuses look good in the snow.

MANICURING is a form of lawn-care maintenance followed by overly compulsive people. Anyone who manicures his lawn should not be left alone lest he mow his fingernails.

TREES are very large green plants similar to shrubs as they are also round, square or pointed in shape. Trees, however, have long "trunks" under their round, square or pointed portions. Novice homeowners (especially those who have recently moved to the suburbs from the city) often purchase and plant many trees on their property with little or no thought given to autumn, when 2.68 million leaves per tree fall down the same weekend it rains in torrents, clogging sewer drains, gutters and chimneys, and knocking out power lines.

Trees not only need watering, pruning and spraying. They also need cabling, feeding and occasional surgery, which a tree service will gladly perform for you—for a fee, of course.

YELLOW AND CLEAR PLASTIC STRIPS are one of the latest trees fads to hit the county in the last decade. Sticky on both sides, these strips encircle tree trunks like snappy new belts, and are a lovely accessory for anyone's yard. For about two weeks in the summer, they function as catch-alls for myopic gypsy moths. The strips' charming ability to flap delicately in the breezes must be the reason most homeowners leave them up, and so they remain—season after season—catching bird droppings, gum wrappers and some of those 2.68 million leaves.

LAWN FURNITURE generally includes chaises, tables, chairs and hammocks that are lugged out of the garage each spring and dragged back inside every fall. This furniture is never used by gardeners, but is in constant service, with joggers, bicyclists, sports enthusiasts and automobile drivers taking short breaks from their hectic routines.

The New York Times — May 8, 1983

A PLACE TO STOP ALONG THE WAY

When I was in the third grade, and able to walk to school by myself, I would start by crossing the playground outside our apartment house, and then turn back to wave good-bye to my grandmother. It was a tiny, brief ritual that she and I enacted—something I could count on as a way to start my day away from home. Grandma always watched me from the kitchen window, and her eyes fell on me like a sweet benediction.

I never told her that I felt edgy leaving home; after all, hadn't she and my mother said I was old enough and "ready?" The first years, my older brother had held my hand and accompanied me, until he entered junior high, which was in a different direction.

"You'll be fine," my grandmother would say cheerfully, as she zipped up my jacket and handed me my lunch box. "When you come home, I want to hear all about your day, what you did, and what you saw."

We hugged each other, and I left. I was uneasy at first, but once I got going, I did feel fine. It was the leaving that was difficult for me—not being away.

Grandma often encouraged me to tackle difficult things by offering sympathetic and wise words of support. "I give up!" I'd snap, when struggling to find the right pieces to fit in a jigsaw puzzle. "They all seem the same to me!"

"Look for all the pieces with one straight side or two, which form a corner," she'd suggest. "They make up the border and are easy to spot. After you do the border, you can figure out what goes where in the middle."

Her advice worked well regarding homework, too—especially arithmetic. Usually, I'd scan the entire page of my work sheet before I began, and throw my hands up in frustration after seeing the final and most complicated problem. "I can't do this! It's too hard!" I'd declare.

"Start at the beginning," she'd say. "Sometimes, the first problems offer clues that help you solve the later ones. Just do as much as you can, and the rest will fall into place."

Each day, during my 2½ block walk to school, I'd subdue my pangs of trepidation (and occupy myself) by observing the trees along my route and studying their shapes and leaves. I looked at lindens, locusts, oaks, and a variety of maples. My favorite was a Norway maple planted on a grassy stretch between the sidewalk and the curb, about two-thirds of the way to school. Reaching it signified that I was almost there.

"My tree"—which I soon called it—was lofty and tall, with a gracefully round shape and narrowly ridged bark. Dense clusters of yellow flowers burst from its boughs in the spring, and were followed by masses of green leaves that turned a gorgeous yellow-orange every fall. In the wintertime, I examined the intricate designs made by the bare branches, and thought they were as lovely as lacework. Like a silent, dependable bystander, my tree watched me come and go.

Years later, after I became a mother, the September days in which my older son, Edward, began elementary school were milestones in my life, as well as his. Bright-eyed and eager, wearing a new shirt, new pants, his hair neatly combed and face freshly washed, he waited at our front door for two older kids who lived down the street and always passed our house. As the kids went by, Edward trailed behind them. He was excited, but also nervous; coming home was easy, but leaving was hard. I knew the feeling very well.

Fortunately, by the end of the first week, Edward had found his own personal link between home and school. He had made friends with "Officer Joe."

Officer Joe was a crossing guard and retired policeman who stopped traffic with his white-gloved hand as he shepherded children across the busy road that separated our neighborhood from the school. Perhaps he sensed my son's uneasiness, or maybe he was equally kind to every child he saw. Whatever the reason, Joe would greet Edward with a hearty "Hi Sport!" as the little boy hurried along. Patting him softly on the shoulder, Joe would confront him by adding, "Okay, kid, you're almost there!"

One afternoon, before school was dismissed, I put my younger son, Peter, in his stroller and pushed it to the corner to see Joe. Instinctively, he raised his hand toward the approaching cars, until he realized we had reached our destination. As I thanked him for helping Edward adjust to leaving home, I said his job was much greater than directing traffic: Joe was an important way station for Edward and, I suspected, other children too.

"Your son's going to be fine," Joe said confidently. "Over the years, I've seen dozens of little ones go by with worried looks on their faces, so I do whatever I can to cheer them up." Chuckling, he added, 'They never look worried when they're heading for home!"

Leaving home and returning are powerful concepts for all of us. Whenever I reminisce about my favorite tree and Officer Joe, I also think about Janus, the ancient Roman deity with two faces—one looking forward and the other looking back. Our lives are filled with beginnings and endings, but they are connected, too. "Go as far as you can, and the rest will fall into place," said my grandmother.

Letting go is never easy, whether it's seeing your child off to school around the corner, or to college across the United States. But as every parent (and grandparent) knows, in order for our children to advance and grow, we have to step back, and away.

Victoria — September/October 2009

A NEW BROOM SWEEPS CLEAN— EXCEPT WHEN A HOUSE IS INVOLVED

"Broom clean," our lawyer said, shortly before my husband and I purchased our new home. "That's the standard way in which a house is left when owners vacate, and you're ready to close the deal."

I was surprised to hear that anyone used a broom anymore. Silently, I wondered, shouldn't the words be "vacuum cleaner clean," or "dust-buster clean?" Sweeping floors seemed quaint, like using a rake instead of a deafening power blower to blast leaves and debris off your lawn.

Okay, I thought. Broom clean is how the house will be. But later, I learned that no matter how empty a house looks after it's sold, stuff remains. And sometimes, it takes an enormous effort for new owners to dispense with the ghosts of owners past.

Maybe it's impossible to get rid of everything, like lint in the dryer or coat hangers tangled on a closet floor. Or maybe sellers think they're being kind and/or helpful by leaving behind open bottles of pesticide, and spray cans of perfumey cleaners. Maybe they were so in love with that broken-down toaster and hall lamp with a tattered shade that they actually thought they were doing you a service by bequeathing these objects to you.

You wish you had stopped them before keys were passed. "No!" you would have wailed. "Take that rusted gas grille with you! Get it out of here!" What one person considers a precious treasure is another person's out-and-out junk.

Several weeks before we moved in, the sellers asked if there was anything we wanted. "Garden equipment would be great," we said, since we knew they were moving to a condo with no lawn. We were thinking of shovels, sprinklers, hedge trimmers and usable outdoor furniture, but what we got was a motley collection of rusted lawn chairs with sagging seats, and a horrifying array of insect powders with blurry labels. To make matters worse, the local dump classified the powders as "hazardous waste" and charged us an "environmental fee" to dispose of them.

A few years before the house went on the market, the sellers' teenage son had slapped acid green day-glo paint on the walls, ceiling, doors and window frames of his room. The place literally glowed in the dark. We covered the noxious color with two coats of thick white paint, and painted it again to make sure it was dead and gone. But whenever one of us bumps into any of the painted surfaces, flecks of that putrid hue reappear and stick out like a bullfrog's tongue.

Remnants of the former owners (and their former lives) continued to pop up in surprising places: under the kitchen sink, where we discovered three bags of moldy Halloween candy; and on a high shelf in the guest room, where a dust-covered corset languished as if it were still mourning the death of FDR.

Then, in the bare master bedroom closet, my husband and I spied a band-aid taped at eye level to the back wall. We stared at the band-aid and giggled. "What do you think would happen if we removed it?" I asked.

"Maybe the house will fall down," my husband joked. But we were curious, and he was willing to take a chance. Gently, he lifted one corner and peeled it off. Nothing happened, but we did see a row of penciled numbers: "34—5—28."

"Looks like the code for a combination lock."

"Maybe it's for a safe. Maybe that's where they stashed the 'family jewels.'"

That was quite a while ago. We're still looking for the safe.

Hartford Courant — June 24, 2007

SUMMER NIGHTS
OF GREAT SWEETNESS

It wasn't until after we purchased our summer cottage on Martha's Vineyard that we realized we could see the Fourth of July fireworks from an upstairs window. Although the display was visible only above a line of trees, we thought it was amazing – especially because it was an unexpected gift.

So, rather than head to the harbor in Edgartown, we stayed home, made popcorn and carried it upstairs to our splendid little vantage point in a guest bedroom. The grownups sat on the beds while the children bunched together merrily by the window sill, clapping their hands and rejoicing after every thunderous boom and blaze of lights.

The Vineyard was originally settled by the Wampanaog Indians, who called the island *Noe-pe*, which means "amid the waters." Located seven miles off the coast of Massachusetts, it was renamed in 1602 by the English explorer, Bartholomew Gosnold, for his infant daughter, and for the wild grapes he found growing in abundance.

Vineyarders have been celebrating Independence Day with revelry and jubilation since 1777, when a "privateer sloop" sailed into Edgartown harbor and fired its cannons, frightening a white horse that ran off "as for life, the saddle and pillion fluttering in the breeze," according to an onlooker. For more than a century, red, white and blue

American flags, streamers and buntings have been draped from the porches and balconies of white Greek Revival houses in Edgartown, gray and white clapboard homes in Vineyard Haven, and the multi-colored, exuberantly painted "gingerbread" houses of Oak Bluffs. On the fourth of July, fireworks are set off from a barge anchored off the coast by Edgartown Lighthouse, and can be seen for miles.

We had bought the cottage in late May, and watching the festivities high over Edgartown harbor and Nantucket Sound became the first summertime ritual we enjoyed, and still do.

Long after sunset, on other nights, the wide-open sky glitters brilliantly. Like its sister islands, Nantucket, and the string of tiny Elizabeth islands, the Vineyard is surrounded by dark blue waters, with virtually no reflective light from the ground to dim our view of the heavens. On pitch black, cloudless nights, the sky is lit up with galaxies of stars.

All this is (more than) enough to routinely awaken me around three a.m., wrap myself in a shawl, and tiptoe to the sliding door in the hallway, which opens on to the deck. The night is pleasantly cool and breezy when I step outside, and I'm alone with the stars and constellations. Dotted like sprinkled sugar on the immense, inverted bowl of sky are: *Ursa Major* – The Big Dipper; *Ursa Minor* – The Little Dipper; *Polaris*, the North Star; *Cassiopeia* in her chair; her daughter, the chained princess *Andromeda*; and *Perseus*, who rescued her.

"The stars are wide and alive, they seem each like a smile of great sweetness, and they seem very near," wrote poet James Agee, remembering nights of his childhood, in "Knoxville: Summer of 1915."

In the dazzling, awesome celestial sphere above me, I believe I can hear subtle, euphonious vibrations of the luminous stars. It's silent, but I can sense what ancient astronomers, mathematicians, and poets throughout the ages have described as "the music of the spheres," when planets revolve in our solar system, whooshing through space in perfect harmony and grace.

Truly, it is a wonderment. If I'm lucky, I will see a shooting star, and make a wish. For what? To come back here, to Martha's Vineyard, again and again.

Victoria — July/August 2009

THIEVES LIKE US

I'm tired of being hassled because of other people's criminal tendencies. I hate two-way mirrors in dressing rooms, patrolling "security personnel," and cameras blinking at me from the corners of banks. I hate checking my bags at the entrance to a shop. I used to enjoy trying on clothes in department stores until they started putting plastic doodads on everything. Those doodads slap my legs and scrape my neck. They are particularly irksome when dangling from a blouse, making it impossible to tuck in and zip up your skirt properly. Besides, that lumpy doodad makes my hips bulge more than they do already.

Yes, yes, I know why sellers of everything from lingerie to luggage do what they do: People steal things. I'm told that the inconvenience of doodads is the price we pay to maintain a civilized existence. But deterrents make life difficult. And often, they don't even work.

I once bought a new coat in a department store and didn't notice the still-attached doodad until I got home. No bells rang when I passed through the exit, but boy, did they go off when I returned! Who paid for my trouble? Just me. I had to drive ten miles round-trip to go back to have the doodad removed!

It's not just clothes. Driving home from work recently, I stopped at a supermarket to pick up bread and a quart of milk. Then I couldn't resist grabbing a bag of onions, two bottles of apple juice, some cans of soup and a dozen oranges, and tossing them into my grocery cart, too. But once I got on the checkout line, I remembered why I hated shopping here: A fence outside the store prevents customers from pushing their carts to their cars.

"Please," I asked the checkout person. "Can you pack everything in two bags? It's a long walk to my car."

The checkout person snorted and rolled her eyes toward heaven. "No way!" she answered.

I groaned. "But your cart corral drives me crazy. It's raining cats-and-dogs outside, and I'll be drenched running back and forth from the parking lot to the pickup area. Why can't you knock down that stupid fence so customers can push their carts all the way over to their cars?

"Are you kidding?" she said. "They put up the fence because people steal the carts."

People steal the carts. I don't, but since I didn't want to leave my purchases unattended, I carried three bags (plus my purse, plus my umbrella, which I couldn't open) 200 feet to my car, where I put the bags down on wet, muddy ground, unlocked my car and loaded it.

Because people steal the carts.

The next time I wanted just a few things, I went to a local convenience store where three battered and rusty carts huddled together in one corner. First, I banged my thumb yanking one cart away from the others, and then I got smacked in the head by a dented metal pole clamped to one side of the basket. When I pushed the cart, it veered to the right. I wrenched it left, and the pole hit my head again. So I struggled down the aisle, pushing the cart with one hand and using the other to push the pole away from me.

"Having trouble?" asked the deli man.

"I sure am," I snapped. "I suppose you're going to tell me that this pole's stuck on the cart to prevent people from stealing this dilapidated piece of junk!"

"You bet!" he said. "People are always trying to steal our carts!" Right. And they're going to use them as Christmas gifts.

Maybe the department store people should talk to the markets people, who could attach those doodads to grocery carts. Whenever would-be thieves attempted to push the carts past parking-lot boundaries, ear-splitting alarms would go off. There would be no way to stop the noise unless the carts were brought back to the store or beaten to death on the sidewalk.

I don't steal carts—or any other kind of merchandise. When I enter a store, I'd like the simple courtesy and opportunity to make a quick purchase.

Shoplifting probably declines when it's not so easy to commit, but there have got to be better ways to reduce the chances without annoying, injuring, and otherwise inconveniencing trustworthy folks—who are, I'm convinced, the majority of shoppers in this world.

Family Circle — June 23, 1991

WORK ETHICS

These days, careful craftsmen have been largely replaced by people in a hurry who do a sloppy job. They are basically decent folks, willing to redo things if you aren't satisfied. They come back to fix the sink... again. Repaint the living room. Rebuild the porch. "Don't worry," they say. "If you're not happy, I can always touch things up." But doing something right the first time beats doing it again any day of the week.

And so we, as consumers, suffer—but we're partly to blame. We accept things we don't want and tolerate second-rate work because we're too busy or worn out to deal with it. We ourselves often rush through jobs and settle for mediocre results. Our days are chopped up into tinier and tinier bits, and "doing the best we can" has come to mean doing as good a job as possible in a very limited time. It's "good enough," we say. Besides, mistakes can be covered up with glue, touch-up paint, or half-closed eyes.

This attitude has backfired on us. We're so used to expecting a new appliance or piece of electronic equipment to break down that most of us automatically buy extended warranty contracts for our purchases. When something arrives broken because the delivery people dropped it, the store owner files an insurance claim while we wait weeks for a replacement. When the cheese hors d'oeuvre marked "good until Sept" is moldy when we unwrap it in May, we're the ones who have to take it back to the store, even if guests are arriving any minute.

Not long ago, my friend returned a new telephone to the shop where she had bought it. "The touch-tone buttons stick when I press them," she told the manager.

"No problem," he said, refunding her money. Two hours later, she saw the same phone in the window again.

"You could make a call with it," she reflected. "I guess he figured someone else wouldn't notice the defect."

I'd notice.

Last week, I picked up a milk container in a food store. The bottom of the carton was wet, so I picked up another. Wet too. After checking half a dozen more, I found the dairy man. "All these cartons are leaking," I told him.

"Oh, no," he answered, smiling. "They're just wet because the shelf is wet. Take what you need," he offered magnanimously. "If you have any problems, you can always bring it back."

Bring it back? I do my marketing once a week, usually on my way home from work. After I lug in six bags of groceries and put them away, I have to make dinner and dash to a PTA meeting. I certainly don't need milk dripping all over my refrigerator. And I don't need to make another trip to the store.

Every Saturday morning, a rolled-up "newspaper" filled with ads is hurled on to my lawn. I never asked anyone for this paper, and I never read it. So I called the company that sends it and asked to be crossed off the list. "To tell the truth, that'll be hard," said the dispatcher. "They guys we hired don't have time to remember who doesn't want a paper delivered."

"Don't say this 'rag' is 'delivered,'" I replied. "It's thrown on my lawn; I call it littering. So figure out some way to stop your 'guys' from doing it."

"I don't know what you're so upset about," he answered. "We haven't had any complaints before. Besides, if you don't want it, just throw it away."

Big deal. I could "throw it away." He thought he was being reasonable. He'd had no complaints because most people don't bother.

Why don't we take our feelings of frustration—and the headaches they produce—and dump them on the people responsible? It's time for store owners and manufacturers to realize that customers returning spoiled food, sending things back to be repaired, rehiring workmen to correct sloppy jobs, won't save any of us time or increase anyone's profits.

In the "good old days," people coped with outdoor plumbing and without TV. There are very few things I'd like to resurrect from that era—but a job done right the first time is one of them.

Family Circle — November 5, 1991

DIGITAL CLOCKS: PRECISION WITHOUT PAST OR FUTURE

"It's 7:58:20," my husband said one morning. He used to say, "It's almost eight o'clock," and let it go at that. But now we are the owners of a digital alarm clock, and speak of time in more exact terms. Digital clocks eschew vagueness, and refuse to acknowledge the past or the future. We can't look at a digital clock and say, when the hands move to "there," Jim will be home or the cake will be done. All we can see is the present moment—the present thin sliver of time.

Today, accuracy is the main objective in selling timepieces. Watches are sold with the guarantee that they will lose only one second every century. The New York Telephone Company recommends I call them each day to learn the exact time because they have something called an atomic clock which won't gain or lose more than one second in 300,000 years. "As a busy New Yorker," their advertisement tells me, "you deserve no less."

What if I want less? What if I'm content to know it's around two o'clock, or going on six? Every appointment isn't a life-and-death situation. Even if I catch a plane with only one minute to spare, it rarely gets going less than ten minutes after its scheduled departure. And show me one hair salon in America that doesn't make you wait at least twenty minutes—no matter how early you get there.

Digital clocks may make some folks more punctual. All they do is make me tense. I prefer face clocks, which tell time more subtly. Just try to slip into the office a few minutes late one morning. If your boss looks up to check the time, a friendly face clock will casually bend its hands in for you just a little, but the digital clock will brazenly proclaim, "9:04:20—9:04:30...."

Time seems to be moving faster these days, now that's broken down into tiny segments. French scientists, I'm told, have determined the existence of chronons, which they describe as the indivisible "atoms" of time, its smallest units. But my new awareness of all those chronons whizzing by doesn't help me spend my time any more wisely than before. My head reels with the nerve-wracking need to fill every second—and fill it fast—before it passes by. Three hundred years ago, a clever French lady named Mme. de Sevigne wrote, "I wouldn't want a watch with a hand that showed seconds; it would chop one's life too fine." And she didn't even know about atomic clocks!

Thousands of years ago, at the earliest beginnings of "recorded" time, people were content to tell time by glancing at a stick in the ground every now and then, and noting its shifting shadows as the sun moved across the sky. This eventually led to sundials, hourglasses, and mechanical clocks.

For centuries, at the sounding of an hour, villagers around the world would look up and see little wooden men and women—or even a small stone animal—hobble out of peekaboo doors to strike miniature anvils, gongs or other reverberators, and announce with great formality the passing of time. Grandfather clocks also "told" time with an aura of great authority.

My neighbors' house is bare. They have thrown out (or carefully hidden) all their mementos, and live among slick Formica tables, lean white sofas, and a couple of indoor trees. Houses such as theirs, furnished in "up-to-the-minute" styles, have no room for what some people call "knick-knacks"—the homey clutter of collectibles which reveal their owners' pasts and private lives. Digital clocks almost seem to make sense in such homes, because they, too, are only concerned with the present.

In my house, the lumpy clay duck my son once made in kindergarten, the indefatigable houseplant that's stuck by us through four moves and thirteen years of marriage, and the soft but faded floor mat which our dog regards as his favorite bed are vital to our self-images. Like the face clock on the mantel, they show us where we've been and help us know who we are.

I think I'll bring our digital clock next door. They can have it as a timely house gift.

Newsday — 1979

FICTION

Ellis Island main building 1919,
courtesy Everett Collection at Shutterstock

ELLIS ISLAND HANUKKAH

On the December night in 1900 when Raisel Rifke's Mama packed her family's bags, a full moon was shining above their home in Galicia. Raisel was not asleep. How could she sleep when tomorrow Mama, Raisel, her younger brother Jacob, and little sister Golda would leave the village where they had lived since they were born? How could anyone sleep when soon they would be on a ship sailing to America, where Papa was waiting for them? His last letter said he would see them by Hanukkah.

Raisel was ten years old, and she remembered watching Mama pack Papa's clothing in a bundle before he left last summer, and how Papa's beard tickled her neck when he kissed her goodbye. "How will Papa find us?" she asked Mama yesterday. "Is he in New York? Where is New York?"

"Shush!" Mama said. "No more questions now."

"But you always say asking questions is good," said Raisel.

"Questions are good, *tokhter*, when there is time for answers, which I do not have," Mama said as she wrapped apples, cheese and bread for them to eat on their journey. "Or if it's an emergency, and you must know right away." She raised her eyebrows and looked closely at her daughter. "So?" Mama asked. "*Iz es a noytfal*?" "Is it an emergency?"

"No," said Raisel softly. She was sad about leaving home, but happy about going to America. Did Mama feel that way too? Since it was not an emergency, Raisel did not ask.

That afternoon, neighbors had come to say goodbye, and patted the family's steamship tickets, called *shifskarten*, for good luck. Everyone looked with curiosity at a pamphlet written in several languages, which was handed out at the local ticket office, and described what travelers could expect on their journeys. Moshe the milkman said it was good that Mama and Raisel knew German as well as Yiddish because speaking German would help them in the outside world. Then he gave Mama a wooden dreidel he had carved "for your first Hanukkah in America." Chana Soura, who lived next-door, took Jacob's cat, Mazel, and promised to care for it. "They say that people in America help each other," she said. Raisel read the pamphlet over and over again, so she could help Mama whenever necessary.

After traveling for days on foot and by train, Mama and the children arrived at Antwerp harbor where the steamship, *Vaderland*, was rocking in the water. Black smoke belched from the highest deck as Mama carried Golda up the gangplank, and Raisel and Jacob followed. Aided by a translator who stood nearby, a crewman wrote down passengers' names and assigned numbers to them. The numbers were attached to tags that passengers had to wear on strings around their necks.

"*Auf zu Amerika!* We are off to America!" everyone shouted from the decks.

That night, Raisel, Mama, Jacob and Golda snuggled together in a crowded and stuffy section of the ship called "Steerage." It smelled like onions, pickled herring, perspiration, and wet baby clothes. Some passengers were snoring, groaning, or nursing babies. Raisel wanted to ask Mama why an old woman was crying, but Mama was rocking Golda, and it was not an emergency.

* * *

After twelve days at sea, *Vaderland* arrived in New York harbor on December 19th. Ships' bells bonged, and fog horns blared as Raisel and her family raced to an open deck. Faint glimmers of lights blinked from nearby ships, and murky images of buildings were glimpsed through the morning mist.

"They'll be calling us 'immigrants' now," a tall woman told Mama. "We have left our homes and come to a new place to live." The woman spoke an interesting mixture of Yiddish, German, and—Raisel believed—English, too.

Inside the Great Hall of the vast red brick Immigration Center, people were talking or hollering in many languages. Others were dazed and silent. Immigration agents in blue uniforms ordered them to form lines according to the numbers on their tags, and directed them up to the Registry Room. Raisel wondered why doctors kept staring at them as they climbed the stairs. "It's to see if we are *shtarkers*— strong and healthy," said the tall woman.

Children over two-years-old had to walk by themselves; they couldn't even hold their mothers' hands! Golda howled for Mama who was across the room until Mama reached in her pocket and pulled out Moshe's *dreidel*. "Come here,

Golda, this is for you," she called brightly. Fighting back tears, Golda rushed to Mama, and fell into her arms.

A kind-looking immigration agent named Mr. McCarthy smiled at Golda. But he frowned when he touched her hot forehead. "What's wrong with her?" he asked Mama. A translator explained his question to her, and she insisted it was "just a slight fever, nothing serious...." Everyone knew that sick passengers could be sent back to Antwerp.

Next, an inspector appeared. "What's wrong with your little girl?" he asked sternly. Again, the translator helped them.

"*Nicht*! It's nothing!" Mama repeated, but her voice was high-pitched and shrill. People gawked at them, and Golda cried again.

"If they think she's sick, why don't they help her get well?" Raisel asked Mama.

"Shush!" Mama scolded. But this was an emergency. Raisel looked at the inspector, whose face was not friendly like Mr. McCarthy's.

"Can't they help my sister?" she asked the translator. "I thought people in America help other people."

The inspector glared at Raisel when her words were repeated to him. He was surprised by her boldness, and he whispered something to Mr. McCarthy. Quickly, the family was taken to a room full of cots, where Golda was put to bed. Mama sent Raisel and Jacob to the dining hall to get food for them. They liked the new taste of bananas, after someone showed them how to peel them first!

Raisel and Jacob were spinning the *dreidel* in a hallway when Mr. McCarthy came along with another translator.

"How is your sister?" Mr. McCarthy asked.

"Much better!" Raisel said brightly, although Golda seemed about the same. Both men wondered about the dreidel.

"It's a Hanukkah game," Jacob explained.

"What does Hanukkah mean?" the agent asked.

Raisel described the time in Jerusalem long ago, when the evil king Antiochus wouldn't let Jews practice their religion, and ordered his soldiers to destroy the Hebrew Temple. At last, the Jews drove away the soldiers, and cleaned and rebuilt the Temple. Although there only was enough oil to burn for one day, it lasted for eight. They were called the eight days of Hanukkah—the Festival of Light and Re-dedication—which Jews have celebrated ever since.

Jacob pointed to the Hebrew letters on the dreidel. "'*Nun*,' '*gimel*,' '*hei*' and '*shin*' stand for the words, '*Nes Gadol Hayah Sham*:' A great miracle happened there," he said proudly. "The Menorah was lit again in the Temple."

Mr. McCarthy nodded. "It sounds like what happens here on Ellis Island. No battles, of course," he added, smiling. "But this building opened just the other day. The previous one was made of wood and burned down three years ago. This place is much safer, because it's made of fireproof brick and steel. There were dedication ceremonies on Opening Day, and more than 2,000 men, women and children passed through, on their ways to new lives in America.

"Everyone who comes through here is starting over," he continued. "They have the chance of a new beginning, a re-dedication, as you call it."

* * *

The family remained on Ellis Island for five days while Mama cared for Golda until she was well. At sunset each day, Raisel and Jacob recited Hanukkah blessings and lit candles with other Jews in the dining hall. At night, they slept in the Registry Room. The sky was dark because there was no moon.

Papa arrived on the last day of Hanukkah. First he hugged Mama. Then he hugged his children, one by one. His beard tickled Raisel's neck.

Mr. McCarthy tipped his cap "Goodbye" as the family sailed away from Ellis Island on a barge. Mama hugged Raisel and told Papa, "If not for Raisel's courage to speak up, we might have been sent back across the sea. Let me tell you—that was a real emergency!"

One of five stories selected and read nationwide on
NPR-member radio stations December 2018

MOLLY'S MENORAH

Dena opened the living room windows in her new home as soon as she came in from work. Almost sixty degrees on Hanukkah! Back in New York, she'd be wearing a heavy coat, boots and a hat already. Here in Atlanta, children played outside all winter long. Molly would love it!

Dena's ten-year-old daughter was still in New York with her grandmother. Molly had been sleeping at Mama's since the day after Thanksgiving, when Dena and Charlie kissed them goodbye and drove to Atlanta to start new jobs.

"Grandma Anna will put you on a plane to join Dad and me in a few weeks," Dena had explained. "As soon as your school's winter vacation begins."

Molly began to cry and hugged Dena especially hard.

"But what about Hanukkah, Mommy?" Molly had asked. Her dark eyes and hair were just like Charlie's. She looked particularly like him when she was upset.

"This time, it will be different, sweetheart. Just you and Grandma."

Mama had been happy when Molly moved in. She always stayed at Mama's apartment after school, anyway, until Dena or Charlie picked her up after work. And if Mama regretted everyone not being together for Hanukkah, at least she didn't say so.

And yet, Dena did feel badly. Mama always said you never miss home until you leave it. But this was silly! Dena had been thrilled about moving south. Living expenses were lower, and salaries were at least as high as they had been in New York. She glanced at a pile of wallpaper rolls and paint supplies stacked in a corner of the dining room. She and Charlie would be busy every night this week, fixing up their new home. No time for Hanukkah this year, but honestly, the holiday had never meant that much to her. Not like it did to Mama and Molly.

Even so, they always went to Mama's on the first night. Mama fried latkes and cooked brisket, and Molly put the Hanukkah candles in the menorah and placed it by the living room window. Dena helped by setting the table, and Charlie played songs like "Light One Candle" on his guitar.

Dena unrolled several feet of the new wallpaper and taped it to a wall. Against a creamy white background, lacy tendrils of ivy twirled around tiny purple flowers. She had chosen well; the colors were glorious.

Mama had been Molly's age when she had brought the beautiful brass menorah with her to America in 1938. The menorah was tall and graceful, with four candle holders on each side. In the middle was a holder for the *shammas* candle, which was used to light the eight Hanukkah candles one by one, on each successive night. Mama always said she loved the *shammas* – or "worker" – candle most, even though it was not a true Hanukkah light. "If not for the *shammas*, none of the Hanukkah lights could be kindled," she explained.

Molly loved polishing the menorah, so it glistened in the candlelight. But she disliked touching Mama's other menorah, which was small and stumpy and made of clay. Its surface was rough and the little cups for oil or candles were blackened and sooty. The little clay menorah stood on a high shelf, and hadn't been lit in years. Maybe she should have told Molly about it, Dena thought. She'd always meant to wait until Molly was older.

Charlie should be home soon, she realized, and she switched on a few lights. This time of year, it got dark so early. When she was a little girl, she'd ask, "When will it be time to light the Hanukkah candles?" and Mama always laughed, saying long ago, she and her little sister, Malka, used to ask their mother the same question and she always said, "As soon as you see three stars in the night sky." That was easy to do in the Carpathian Mountains of Bukovina, Romania, but in New York City there were so many lights, who could see the stars?

Mama had told her about her childhood in eastern Europe, and how rumors of trouble for the Jews began trickling in when she was very young. Mama said she actually had two childhoods: the one "before," and the one "after."

Her father, Abraham, had once been a wonderful story teller, especially at Hanukkah time before the "troubles" started. He told his children about the Maccabees, who fought the evil King Antiochus who demanded that everyone follow his religion. The Maccabees said people could live together in peace, even if they didn't have the same religion. That's the way it was in America, Abraham said, and shortly before Hitler's army marched east, he arranged for Anna to go to America with other people from their village. He, his wife Dora and little Malka would follow later, after Abraham had sold his dry-goods shop and most of their belongings.

Mama never forgave herself for leaving Malka behind. "I should have insisted, but the people who took me didn't want young children," she told Dena many times. "They only let me come along because I could take care of myself."

She lived with her Aunt Ettie in New York, and waited for her parents and Malka to come soon. But nine years passed until her father arrived, broken-hearted and alone. His sadness lifted for a while, later on, when Anna married her beloved Jacob, whom she had met in college. Dena's father was a joyous man, but he had died five years ago. She remembered her grandfather only as a weary old man who rarely smiled. The only times Abraham brightened were when he talked of life in Bukovina with his daughters and his dear wife, after whom Dena was named.

Molly had been named in memory of Malka; had Dena ever told her that it was a Jewish tradition to name babies after deceased relatives? Had it been wrong, also, to keep her daughter in the dark about all the suffering of her grandmother's family? Even Charlie knew only a little. She began setting the table for dinner. Why bring up the past when the future was so bright?

Charlie came home a half hour late; he'd been trying to buy Hanukkah candles. "I must have looked in five different stores," he said. "But no luck. Three shopkeepers said they didn't stock them, and the others said they had sold out. I'm sorry."

"That's okay," said Dena. She was surprised he had thought of it. "I'm not sure I could find our menorah. It's still in one of the packing crates."

"It's not okay with me," Charlie grumbled. He had Molly's worried expression on his face. "It's Hanukkah time, but Molly's not here, your mother's not here, and now, we can't even light our menorah—wherever it is."

"I think I can find our wine glasses," Dena said brightly. "We can make a Hanukkah blessing."

New neighbors had given them a bottle of wine as a housewarming gift. Charlie uncorked it and they raised their glasses. Darkness had fallen, making long soft shadows over the newly arranged furniture and packing crates.

"Praised be you, *Adonai*, who sanctifies us with Thy commandments, who performed wondrous deeds for our ancestors in days of old at this season, and who commands us to kindle the Hanukkah lights... even though we can't find them," sang Charlie. His voice was sweet and tender and suddenly, Dena felt bereft and lonely. They sat at the kitchen table and sipped their wine slowly. Grandpa Abraham used to say we carry memories of our homes and our loved ones in our hearts, no matter how far away we go.

"I've put off sharing Mama's stories for too long," Dena told Charlie. "You already know that she came to America before the Nazis got to Bukovina. That's when her parents took little Malka to a farm nearby, before they went into hiding. On a farm, they thought Malka could have something like a normal life. The farmers weren't Jewish, but taking care of Jewish child was a dangerous thing to do."

Charlie nodded sympathetically, and Dena knew he was thinking of Molly. Could they ever part with her that way?

Dena continued: "No one knew my grandmother would die in hiding and Grandpa would be on the run for years, until the war ended and he went back to the farm to get Malka.

"The farmer cried when he told Grandpa what happened. Malka had been a good girl, he said. She helped him and his wife tend the animals and keep the house clean. The first winter, she asked them when Hanukkah was coming. They didn't really know, but they thought it occurred around the time of the winter solstice. Malka wanted a menorah. It seemed so important to her that the farmer said she could make one with clay from the soil behind their house. She made the holes by pressing her fingers into the clay."

"So that's where that menorah came from," said Charlie. "Molly thinks it's ugly, I'm sorry to say."

"So did I, when I was her age," said Dena. "But Malka celebrated three Hanukkahs with it. There were no candles, and very little oil to spare. It probably only burned for a few seconds each night. Then, by the end of the third winter, she grew extremely thin and sickly and ... she died by spring. Later, when my grandfather came to get her, they gave him her menorah. And he gave it to Mama."

Charlie squeezed Dena's hand gently. "I've always meant to tell Molly about it," she said. "But it's such a sad story. What good does it do to tell a child?"

"Molly needs to know," said Charlie. "That menorah ... I want it here, in our home." He sighed deeply, stood up and walked toward the back door. "Let's go outside for a while," he said.

The night air was almost as mild as the day had been. Lamplight glowed softly through the windows; the house looked lovely. Dena took a deep soothing breath and looked up. Two, then three stars glittered. Here, you could see the night sky.

The phone rang and they raced inside to answer it. "Grandma and I just lit the Hanukkah candles," Molly said. "She gave me a special gift, too." Molly sounded terribly grown up, now that she was far away. "I'll let her tell you all about it!"

"Hi darlings," said Mama, who had picked up another receiver. "We miss you tonight, but know you are making a beautiful new home for yourselves." Dena smiled, knowing her mother was saying this for Molly, as much as for themselves.

"You know the little clay menorah? It belongs to Molly, now," Mama said. "I was given the brass menorah when I left my home and started a long journey. Molly, too, will be starting a new life in Atlanta. And since she was named for my dear sister Malka, she should have her menorah. I told her the story of when Malka made it, and you know what? She just told me it's beautiful."

Mama paused. "Our lumpy, little menorah is now beautiful to her," she said.

"Yes, Mama," said Dena. "I know what she means. I also know that next year, we all need to be together when we light the Hanukkah candles. Of course, we hope you'll visit us much sooner," she added quickly. "And often, too. Atlanta's just a few hours away by plane."

Charlie smiled broadly and put his arms around her.

"You know I'll be there," said Mama.

"That's great!" said Molly, who had been listening, too. "Have you and Daddy lit our menorah yet?"

"No, not yet," said Dena. "I've been so busy .... and I can't find it. But it's here somewhere, in one of the shipping boxes."

"Did you look in the boxes sealed with yellow tape?" Mama asked. "The movers used it when they ran out of tape with the company's logo on it. That was the day I stopped by to help and bring lunch, because all the dishes had been packed. I tucked a small box of Hanukkah candles in next to your menorah, and rolled it all up in bubble wrap. I'm pretty sure it's in a box with yellow tape."

Now Dena was in a hurry to get off the phone. "I'll look, Mama," she answered. "Listen, I'll call you later," she said, and hung up.

With steadfast determination, she and Charlie opened and emptied every crate sealed with yellow tape until they found their menorah, with Mama's priceless gift beside it. They inserted candles into the holders, and lit the first Hanukkah light in their new home. Together, they recited the Hanukkah blessing again. Then they set their menorah on the broad window sill in the living room, leaving a space for Molly's menorah, too.

Good Housekeeping — December 2005

AN UNEXPECTED HANUKKAH MIRACLE

Snow was falling softly when Melissa climbed upstairs to the attic of her Connecticut home. She already had purchased most of her family's Hanukkah gifts, and hidden them in a far corner of the attic. Wrapped in festive holiday papers were a fishing rod, DVDs and books for her husband, Dan, and seven gifts for Rosey. But Melissa was still mulling about what to give Rosey on the eighth and final night.

From the top of the stairs, Melissa saw the old trunk she had pulled out after Rosey's 5th grade teacher had announced that their class would be going to Ellis Island. Mrs. Brennan had also asked everyone to find out when their families arrived in America, and where they came from.

"About one hundred years ago, from somewhere in Eastern Europe," Melissa had said. She had a hunch that the trunk might hold more information. All she knew was that around 1900, her great-grandmother Raisel had come with her mother, brother and sister. Melissa guessed that Raisel would have been about Rosey's age.

There had been family stories, mainly forgotten now, about how Raisel's little sister Becky had been sick. There also was a story ... something about Hanukkah. Melissa regretted not knowing Raisel, who died when she was a baby. "She held you when you were born, and called you her link to immortality," her father said. "Looking at you, she said she could see her future."

The family had kept some of Raisel's things, including a woolen shawl and a notebook written in Raisel's plain yet graceful handwriting. Melissa opened the trunk and pulled out the shawl. A small wooden *dreidel* tumbled out, too. Gently, she rubbed her finger over the carved Hebrew letters —"*nun*," "*gimel*," "*hei*," and "*shin*," which stood for the words, "*Nes Gadol Hayah Sham*," and meant "A Great Miracle Happened There." This referred to the Maccabees' battles against King Antiochus, who had desecrated the Temple in Jerusalem and ordered Jews to convert to his religion or be killed. After three years, the Jews reclaimed their Temple, and in 165 B.C.E., the Festival of Lights and Feast of Rededication began.

Putting the shawl over her shoulders, Melissa began reading the notebook:

"December 12, 1969, the last night of Hanukkah: My name is Raisel, and I was born in 1890 in Zbarazh, which is now part of western Ukraine. When I was eight years old, my father left for America. Neighbors patted his steamship ticket for good luck, and wished him a safe trip. He promised to send tickets for us as soon as he could.

"Years later, when my own children were growing up, they seldom asked about my life in Zbarazh, or what happened when I came to America. My grandchildren ask even less. But I have hopes that one of my descendants will want to know everything. By then, I will probably be gone from this world. So this is a love letter to you, dear child of mine who is curious, for you are the one who asks questions..."

Melissa closed the notebook and carried it downstairs. When Rosey came home, she couldn't stop talking about the upcoming field trip. Usually, she didn't talk about schoolwork, which she found difficult. But the topic of family history interested her a great deal, especially because Melissa had agreed to accompany the class. That evening, Melissa and Rosey began reading Raisel's notebook.

"Like you, dear child in the far-off future, I was an inquisitive youngster who asked questions. 'Too many,' Mama said, shushing me when grownups spoke. But it is because I was not afraid to ask an important question that my family and I stayed on Ellis Island."

"Hmmm," Melissa said. "She reminds me of a girl I know."

"But I don't ask questions," said Rosey. "Not in school, anyway. Mrs. Brennan gets annoyed when kids ask what she calls 'unnecessary questions.' If I want to know something, I ask my friend Olivia. She sits near me, and is very smart."

Melissa was silently amused by Rosey's solution, and kissed the top of her head.

"Mama, Jacob, little Becky and I boarded a ship for America two years after Papa left. It was a rough, ten-day voyage, with much seasickness among the passengers. We entered New York harbor on December 21, 1900, and put on our best clothes. Mama wrapped her shawl around Becky because she was shivering. Everyone cheered when we passed the Statue of Liberty, because we knew in America you would be accepted, no matter what your religion or history was. After our ship dropped anchor, we waited to be transferred to Ellis Island.

"Immigration agents directed us up a flight of stairs to the Registry Room. The agents spoke English, most of which we couldn't understand, but we watched them carefully and followed their instructions. Children older than two had to walk by themselves, to show that they were healthy. They couldn't even hold their mothers' hands! Becky cried about this, until a kindly agent in a blue uniform showed her a small dreidel he had found. Mama realized that he was offering it to Becky as a reward if she would walk on her own. So Mama stood with the agent and beckoned to Becky. Fighting back tears, Becky rushed to Mama, and fell into her arms.

"The agent's name was Mr. Flanagan. He smiled and handed the dreidel to Becky. But then he touched her forehead and frowned. Mama knew what he was thinking: Becky was sick with a fever.

"Mr. Flanagan guided us to a line where immigrants were being questioned. Mama spoke German as well as Yiddish, and she managed to communicate with an inspector assisted by a translator. I knew some German, too, and I listened intently. Mama admitted that Becky was sick but insisted it was 'nothing serious....'

"The inspector looked at Becky, and then at Jacob and me as if he suspected that we were sick too. 'What is wrong with your daughter?' he asked Mama sternly.

'It's nothing!' she repeated, her voice rising to a high-pitched sound so shrill that people gawked at us. Her stridency upset me, too, because I feared we'd be put on the next ship back to Europe.

"'If they think she's sick, why don't they help her?' I asked Mama. 'Shush!' she scolded. Then I turned to the

unfriendly inspector and said, 'Are you going to send us back without trying to help my sister get well? I thought people in America try to help other people.'

"The inspector glared at me. I knew that he was angry, but he was also impressed. He whispered something to Mr. Flanagan. Quickly, we were escorted to a room called a dormitory, where Becky was put to bed. Years later, I learned that Ellis Island had no hospital at that time. The best they could do was improvise."

"What's that mean, Mommy? Immmm...." asked Rosey.

"Improvise, sweetheart, means doing the best you can with what you have on hand."

"Like when I ask Olivia for help?" asked Rosey.

Melissa grinned. "Yes, you could call that 'improvising.'"

"'Raisel,' Mama said. 'Take Jacob to the dining hall and eat. Then bring food to me, so I can feed Becky.'

"Jacob and I ate bananas and white bread for the first time in our lives. After we bit into the banana skins, a grownup showed us how to peel them first. We showed Mama and she said we could play with the dreidel in a hall near Becky's room. Mr. Flanagan came along as we were spinning the dreidel.

"'Your sister – how is she?' he asked in broken German.

"'Much better,' I said brightly, although Becky looked the same to me.

"'I hope you can leave here before Christmas day,' he said. 'Best to be only with your family then.' His blue eyes twinkled, as if to say, don't worry.*

"In Zbarazh, I had been afraid of people who celebrated Christmas, but I was not afraid of Mr. Flanagan. Should I tell him we are Jews? I wondered."

"Of course she should," said Rosey. "Everyone knows I'm Jewish!"

"Long ago, people tended not to talk about their religion," Melissa told her.

"Jacob seemed afraid to admit that we were Jews. So I told Mr. Flanagan, 'We are Jews, and we celebrate Hanukkah.'

"He nodded. 'That explains why I see Jewish people lighting candles at sundown,' he said. 'Each night, they light one more, and say Hebrew prayers.'

"With so much happening on Ellis Island, I had no idea that anyone remembered Hanukkah. 'Yes,' I said. 'They are lighting Hanukkah menorahs, (which, actually, are called Hanukkiahs.')

"'So, tell me, what does Hanukkah mean?' he asked, as he leaned back against a railing.

"I thought hard, and tried to remember what Mama and Papa had taught me. I told Mr. Flanagan about the Maccabees and Antiochus, and that after the battles ended, the Jews returned to their Temple, scrubbed it clean, and lit the menorah with oil. It was the 25th day of Kislev, a time of re-dedication and celebration.

"'It sounds a little like what has happened here,' he said. 'This building opened just the other day. It's much safer than the previous wooden one, which burned down three years ago, because it's made of fireproof brick and steel. Dedication ceremonies were held on Opening Day,

as more than 2,000 men, women and children entered the United States.'

"'Everyone who comes through Ellis Island is starting over. 'They have the chance of a new beginning, a re-dedication, as you call it.' Then: 'What does the dreidel have to do with all this?'

"'It reminds us that a great miracle happened long ago,' said Jacob proudly. He showed Mr. Flanagan the Hebrew letters on the sides of the dreidel. 'We spin it and do whatever the letters say.'"

"We also eat jelly doughnuts, and potato pancakes," Rosey interrupted. "And we get eight presents – one on each night!" She paused and looked worried. "But Raisel doesn't talk about presents, Mommy. Maybe she didn't get any."

"Let's keep reading, and see."

"Becky's fever broke on December 25th. Mama cared for her the whole time, and Jacob and I peeked in every day. At dusk, we recited the Hanukkah blessings as candles were lit in the dining hall.

"Mama had been worried about Papa, who would have been checking to see when our ship arrived. Later, we learned that Mr. Flanagan took a ferry to Manhattan on his day-off and went to Papa's home near the dock. He left word for Papa there, to wait a few days before coming to Ellis Island. He arrived on the eighth day of Hanukkah, and we were ready to go!

"In Zbarazh, my Hanukkah gifts had been candy, coins, and pretty mittens that Mama knitted for me. Now, my presents were much greater: Becky recovered; we could stay in America; and Papa brought us to our new

home. Instead of eight gifts on eight nights, we received all these at once. Such was the result of having the courage to be bold and ask important questions!"

On a cold but clear morning, several days later, Melissa, Mrs. Brennan, Rosey and her classmates went to Ellis Island. They toured dormitories, dining halls, baggage rooms, the Great Hall, and the hospital, which opened in 1902. In the Registry Room, Rosey imagined that she was standing exactly where Raisel and her family had stood.

Watching her daughter amble about the room with rapt attention, Melissa wished she had brought her camera to record this scene. Then she realized she didn't need a picture to remember such a day. Sometimes, the best gifts are those we cannot hold. If Raisel hadn't asked for medical help ... if kind Mr. Flanagan hadn't been on duty that week ... if Becky's fever had worsened ... things could have ended badly. There would always be moments of darkness in the world, but brave people would find ways to bring back the light.

Melissa looked at display cases of immigration records, and the rows of wooden benches and inspectors' desks that remained as testaments to all the immigrants who had been here, and she watched Rosey's classmates examining weather-beaten suitcases and steamer trunks, antique clothing and toys, pictures of steamships, and other relevant artifacts.

Rosey walked to a window, where sunlight washed over her like a sweet benediction. Melissa followed, and put her arm around her daughter. Together, they watched seagulls circling the well-worn ferry slip, and small boats bobbing in the water.

"Hanukkah doesn't begin for another week," she told Rosey. "But I think we have received a wonderful gift already."

"What?" asked Rosey.

"Coming to Ellis Island is part of it, but the biggest gift was reading Raisel's notebook with you. It's made today's visit more precious and exciting than I ever could have imagined. Just think – if your class hadn't planned this trip, I wouldn't have opened that old trunk. "

Almost two weeks later, Rosey and her parents lit the eighth candle in their menorah and recited the Hanukkah blessings.

"I wonder if the immigrants on Ellis Island used oil or candles to light their menorahs," said Rosey.

"That's an interesting question," said her father. "Probably, they used both."

"Some people use electric menorahs today," said Melissa. "But the ceremony and story never change." Reaching into her pocket, she pulled out a small package and handed it to Rosey. "Long ago, Raisel said I represented her future. But now it's in your hands, not mine."

Rosey opened the package and stared wide-eyed at the wooden *dreidel* she had read about but never seen. "I thought it was lost. It's Raisel's, isn't it?" she asked.

"It certainly is," said Melissa. "I found it when I discovered her notebook in the attic. After we read about the *dreidel*'s importance, I decided to wait and give it to you. Isn't it the perfect gift to end Hanukkah this year? I hope you will always remember Raisel's story, and tell it again and again – even when you, too, are a great-grandmother."

Rosey hugged the *dreidel* against her chest. "Oh, I love it! And I promise I'll keep it forever. Or at least until I'm a great-grandmother!"

Melissa continued, "You already know that the Hebrew letters stand for *'A Great Miracle Happened There,'* but I also believe that a great miracle happened here in America, when Raisel found the courage to speak up on Ellis Island. If not, her family might have been sent back to Europe. Then Raisel's father would have gone back too. Possibly, they might have stayed, and if that happened, Raisel would never have met her husband, Mendel, in Connecticut and...."

"What would have happened to us?" asked Rosey.

"Now that, my dear daughter, is truly an excellent question!"

First published here, in <u>Counting Heads</u> — 2023

INDEX

Restoring a Pre-Holocaust Torah, and a Family
DOROT—The Journal of the Jewish Genealogical Society — Fall 2020

Rock-and-Roll is a Fundamental
The New York Times — April 23, 1989

Settlement House Spirit Lives On
The Jewish Forward — May 11, 2001

Some Helpful Gardening Hints for Suburban Transplants
The New York Times — May 8, 1983

Star Sightings
The Jewish Week of New York — July 2, 1999

Stories We Never Heard
The Jewish Week of New York — November 18, 2008

Summer Nights of Great Sweetness
Victoria — July/August 2009

Tender Buttons, Tender Memories
Victoria — January/February 2009

The Key to Home
First published here, in <u>Counting Heads</u>

The Soul of Poldek Pfefferberg
The Jewish Week of New York — April 17, 2009

The War on Dirt
American Baby — November 1990

Thieves Like Us
Family Circle — June 23, 1991

To Save One Life
The Jewish Week of New York — May 6, 2005

Tribute to a Manufacturer's Rep Suggests Traits of Success
Furniture Today — May 18, 1985

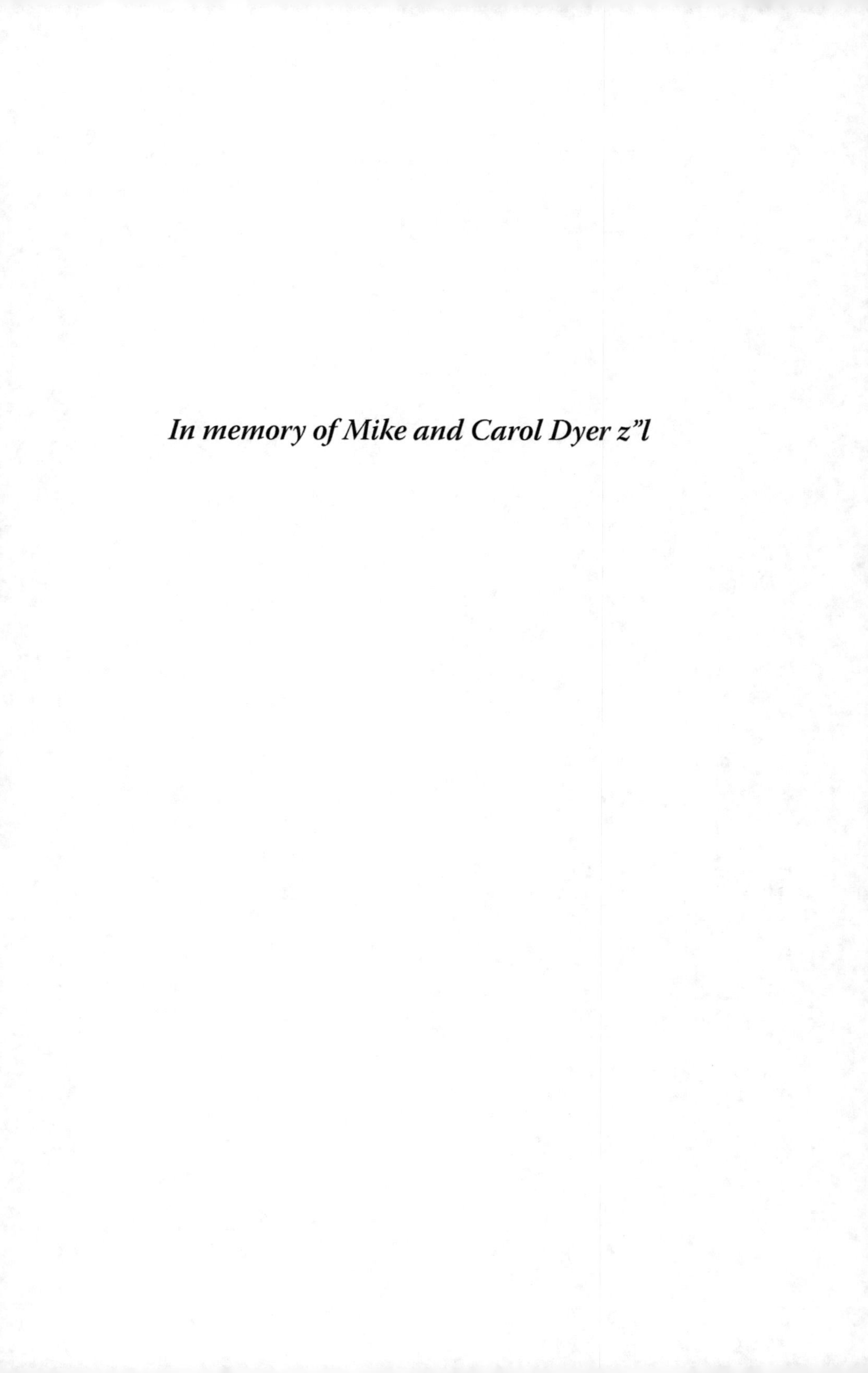

In memory of Mike and Carol Dyer z"l

About the Author

Susan J. Gordon is the author of stories, essays, and articles for many nationally known magazines, newspapers, and online websites including *The New York Times, Family Circle, Good Housekeeping, Woman's Day, Parents*, various genealogical journals, and *Victoria*, where she was Writer-in-Residence. Her non-fiction book, <u>WEDDING DAYS: When and How Great Marriages Began</u>, describes the courtships and marriages of hundreds of famous couples throughout history.

Gordon's award-winning memoir, <u>BECAUSE OF EVA: A Jewish Genealogical Journey</u>, was inspired by painful gaps in her family's history, and tells how still-haunting mysteries in the past compelled Gordon to delve into World War II and Holocaust history.